CARA DEVINE

STRONG, SWEET
AND BITTER

STRONG, SWEET AND BITTER

CARA DEVINE

Hardie Grant

BOOKS

INTRODUCTION

**THE ART OF HOSTING AND THE
FUNDAMENTALS OF FLAVOUR**

It matters not
whether you are
a professional
bartender or simply
a person who makes
drinks for guests at
your home. Your role
is the same. It is that
of 'Mine Host'.

Gary Regan, *The Joy of Mixology*, 2003

The best cocktail I've ever had was a Mango Daiquiri, at a restaurant in Thailand. It was my first proper holiday anywhere in Asia, and first overseas holiday with my fiancé. We were in Ayutthaya, a city known more for its temples than its tipples, and we had walked for what felt like miles in the pitch dark, along a muddy road with little sign of life. It was unbearably muggy and we were hungry and very, very thirsty, so when a restaurant's flashing beer signs loomed ahead like an oasis we knew we were stopping there no matter what – and it turned out to have a beautiful deck at the back by the riverside, friendly staff and cocktails! The rum was ordinary but the mango was fresh, and the drink was the size of my head, frozen and thirst-quenching and the most delicious thing I'd ever tasted (besides the noodles they also served up in heaped quantities!).

A Mango Daiquiri is not my favourite drink, nor an old faithful that I come back to time and time again. I'm talking about my favourite drinking experience, and that is about so much more than what is in the glass. If I asked you to describe the best drink you've ever had, I bet you would tell me a story too – about the drink itself, of course, but also your surroundings, who you were with, how the drink was served and who served it to you.

The purpose of this book is to give you such a thorough grounding in the fundamentals of flavour that you don't have to stress about what's in the glass because you know you can make it delicious. Once you're well acquainted with the Taste Triangle (the foundation of every single cocktail) and understand complementary flavours and how different ratios affect the finished product, it's genuinely hard to make a bad drink! You'll feel confident to smash out classics or whip together a new creation with what you have on hand, and cater to larger groups with ease. Then, you can relax and have fun with your guests – and that's what makes a truly good host.

I fell in love with bartending and drinks culture while sitting at the bar of some consummate hosts. I'd worked in hospitality since I was legally old enough to, but as a part-time job alongside studying Law at university. When I graduated, I decided to take a working holiday before taking the first step on the corporate ladder I expected to be my career. I found myself working in a pre-Prohibition style cocktail bar called Pourhouse in the trendy Gastown area of Vancouver and, from my perch at the door (I was a literal host!), I watched the bartenders being masters of their domain, orchestrating the guest experience with the sole purpose of making them happy. A smile, a chat (or being left alone if that's your mood!), and the perfect drink – it's all anyone really wants at the end of the day, right?

The first time I sat at the bar I was nervous; I felt very unsophisticated in such a suave setting. When I was asked what I wanted to drink, my mind went blank – the only cocktail I could think of was a French Martini. Since that is very much not a pre-Prohibition drink, they were unable to make it for me but let me down with such grace that I felt it was my own decision to try something different. I was given a Gin Sour made with Hendricks and celery bitters, and it was a revelation. I was hooked, and have spent the last 10-plus years bartending and trying to recreate that feeling for my guests. Lots of bars can make you a good drink, but the ones you go back to time and time again are the ones where you feel genuinely welcomed. That is the art of hosting.

After Vancouver I managed to talk myself into a bar job back in Glasgow, in a five-star hotel called The Blythswood Square Hotel. It had an excellent bar program and was very busy, so I learned quickly!

Moving to Australia was eye-opening – the food and drink scene in Melbourne is second to none, and to be immersed in it is infinitely inspiring. My current role is bar manager of a rooftop bar with a Spanish twist, called Bomba, which puts me in charge of staff training (among many other things – not all glamorous!). I've found that sharing my passion for this industry is easily my favourite aspect of the job.

To that end, a couple of years ago I started working on a YouTube channel called *Behind the Bar with Cara Devine* with the aim of demystifying all things bar and booze, and quickly realised one of the things that holds people back from making cocktails (apart from the confidence to give it a go in the first place!) is not having the exact ingredients for a recipe. Never let that stand between you and mixing a drink! I guarantee, with some clever substitutions, you'll be able to concoct something that hits the mark – and is maybe even better than the original.

Bartending is not rocket science, but it is alchemy. The ingredients come together to form the drink; the drink comes together with the atmosphere and the company to create magic. So, without further ado – let's get mixing!

HOW TO USE THIS BOOK

There is a plethora of bartending and booze books available (which my own bulging bookcase can attest to), so why choose this one? Well, I want this to be a one stop shop – more than just a list of recipes. This book deconstructs cocktails to their constituent parts and helps you understand how to put them back together again.

One thing that's important to remember is that bartenders don't hold hundreds of individual recipes in their heads! (Hopefully I don't get my bartender card revoked for shattering that illusion!) There are a few recipe blueprints, all anchored in the three fundamental taste blocks (strong, sweet, and sour or bitter – don't worry, there's plenty more on this coming up), which can be relied upon to produce consistently delicious drinks. Switching out ingredients and playing with ratios is how new drinks are invented, but balance is key. I want to introduce you to these blueprints and show you how to build on them, whether to discover variations on your favourite drinks or construct something new entirely.

This is not a cocktail history book, but the more recent history of the world can be told through cocktails – and that's the kind of lesson I pay attention to! The economic and social climate of the times is often reflected in what people are drinking, so it would be remiss of me not to point out cultural context, tall tales and other interesting titbits where relevant – a good host always has a story or two up their sleeve! I have no problem in saying, though, that not all older recipes included will be historically accurate; I care much more about making a tasty drink than faithfully recreating a century-old recipe. The collective palate changes, as do ingredients, so it's silly to think that older recipes won't need tweaking – but I will always point out where my version departs from the 'classic'.

I have included all the information you need in equipment and technique so you can hit the ground running, but I do believe making good drinks doesn't need to be complicated, so I have stuck to the basics for the most part. Mastering those basics is important though, and often the difference between an ordinary drink and a great one. Chefs might call it *mise en place*, bartenders might call it 'prep', but we can all agree that getting your shit together ahead of time is a good idea. Similarly, making a drink is an act of love, whether for yourself (self-care!) or someone else, so taking the time to make it beautiful is always worth it. I hope that this book will be useful for professional and home bartenders alike, as the majority of the principles espoused within apply equally in both situations.

It would be possible to fill volumes on any given spirit or other cocktail ingredient – in fact, people have! So again, I have included as much detail as I think is relevant to understanding how to utilise each product to best effect, with more emphasis on flavour profiles than getting tied up in the technicalities.

The intention is for this book to be a practical guide to getting the most out of what you have to hand in any given situation – because drinking good booze is one of life's greatest pleasures!

What are you mixing first?

What Drink Should I Make?

When someone walks up to the bar and is unsure what they feel like drinking, I don't say 'do you want a gin drink?' because that's not actually very helpful – a Martini, a Tom Collins and a Red Snapper are all gin drinks but couldn't be more different otherwise! Instead, I always start with the style of drink: 'Do you feel like something tall and refreshing? Short and boozy? Citrusy and fresh? Or a wildcard – creamy, maybe, or savoury?'. From there it is easily narrowed down with a couple of questions about base spirit and other flavour likes/ dislikes – and remember, individual ingredients can almost always be substituted. This is how you should use this book – decide what you feel like, get yourself to the right section and take it from there.

13

CHAPTER ONE

THE FOUNDATION OF EVERY GOOD COCKTAIL

THE TASTE TRIANGLE

Cocktail, then, is a stimulating liquor, composed of spirits of any kind, sugar, water, and bitters.

13 May 1806, *The Balance, and Columbian Repository*, Hudson, New York, USA

This is the earliest written definition of the cocktail and, while at first glance it might not look like it has much in common with '80s disco drinks or modern molecular mixology, it actually lays out the foundations of every successful cocktail – strong, sweet and bitter (or sour). These three elements form the three sides of the triangular base that has underpinned cocktail creativity from 1806 to the present day! I call this the Taste Triangle.

It is important here to differentiate between 'taste' and 'flavour'. We start with the Taste Triangle because 'taste' is a basic sense – it is how your tongue perceives sweet, sour, salty, bitter and umami (savoury), and therefore how it perceives balance. It's mechanical! Flavour is a little more convoluted – it encompasses taste but also specific flavour compounds, aroma, texture and, I would argue, sense-memory to create an overall impression of what you're drinking. This is why I can balance a drink that has an aniseed flavouring even though it is my Kryptonite!

The Taste Triangle can lean more heavily in one direction – some cocktails are a bit sweeter, some a little more sour – but you absolutely cannot miss out one side entirely or the whole cocktail falls down. It might seem a little odd to discuss 'strong' as a taste (and of course it's not in the technical sense of the five tastes that we have flavour receptors for), but it does function as one in cocktails. That underlying boozy punch is integral to a good drink, and the 'strong' ingredient also underpins the other flavours. Without alcohol (or some other substitute that acts as a similar driving force) your cocktails will taste insipid – and no one wants that!

So let's have a look at this terrific trifecta in a bit more detail!

What is Balance?

The alchemy in mixing a cocktail is to make it more than the sum of its parts. No one flavour or sensation should overpower entirely. If, when taking a sip, you find yourself thinking 'too strong', 'too sweet', 'too sour', 'too bitter' – then your drink is unbalanced. Worry not! It can be saved – see page 24.

Cocktail Building Blocks

The Old Fashioned (page 88) is the archetypal cocktail. It has a spirit base forming the 'strong', sugar syrup (sweet) and cocktail bitters (bitter). The bitter element can also be replaced by something sour, as in a Daiquiri (page 112): rum (strong), sugar syrup (sweet) and lime juice (sour), because its purpose is to balance the sweetness, and both have a similar effect.

You can have more complicated drinks too though, where multiple flavour building blocks make up each side of the triangle. For example, the Zombie (page 158) contains several rums (strong), several syrups (sweet), aniseed liqueur (sweet), lime juice (sour), grapefruit juice (sour/bitter) and Angostura bitters (bitter) – phew! You could remove any sweet or any sour or bitter ingredient and the drink would still work, as long as the overall proportions of sweet and sour remained balanced, but you couldn't remove all of the sweet or all of the sour/bitter ingredients and expect it to be enjoyable.

THE THREE SIDES OF THE TASTE TRIANGLE: STRONG, SWEET AND BITTER/SOUR

STRONG

The 'strong' element is the driving force of your cocktail. It's the base – what gives it body and a backbone, underpinning the whole drink. Often referred to as 'spirit base' I prefer 'strong' because, while it often is a spirit, it doesn't have to be. Some cocktails, for example, are based on fortified wines or vermouth instead of a spirit and don't lack a flavour punch! Non-alcoholic spirit replacements can also be used here for a no or low-alcohol option. The strong part of the cocktail does generally have to be dry (i.e. no added sugar), and usually brings a drying effect to the whole drink whether through a savouriness, spice or minerality.

SWEET

'Sweet' is often seen as a dirty word. Too many people have suffered through sticky and sickly cocktail monstrosities in their lifetimes! However, sweetness is an integral part of any cocktail; not only is it the balancing counterpoint to sour and bitter flavours, it also adds body, texture and depth. If you don't believe me, try a Mojito (page 146) without the sugar syrup (sadly, a reasonably common request across the bar). The rum, lime and mint jag across your palate discordantly, and the already thin flavour quickly gets thinner as the ice melts, until you're drinking sour mint water with a hint of ethanol. It's a genuinely upsetting experience, and one I do my best to gently talk guests out of . . . to varying degrees of success depending on their trust issues! Perhaps, as an industry, we deserve this mistrust as atonement for the sins of our syrup-slinging forebears, but most modern bartenders understand the subtlety with which to deploy sweetening agents.

Used judiciously, sugar is the salt of the cocktail world – it enhances desirable flavours while smoothing out any harshness, without being a perceivable taste itself.

BITTER OR SOUR

'Sour' or 'bitter' is the other half of the balancing act – they're not necessarily desirable sensations when isolated, but the interplay between these elements and sweetness are what keep you coming back for more. They add complexity and interest, and all the best cocktails have an aspect of intrigue . . .

Of course, sour and bitter are two very different taste experiences. 'Sour' flavours – i.e. acid – tingle across your palate and send a message to your brain to be on alert, which causes you to salivate. They are, literally, mouthwatering! This is why you might want to smash out bright and citrus-driven drinks on a sunny day – think Margaritas (page 132) or Southsides (page 120).

Bitter flavours hit you at the back of the palate and linger, giving your drinks plenty of length and spice. They usually come from woody botanicals in ingredients like amari or cocktail bitters and often produce the kind of drink to ruminate on in a leather armchair – the Manhattan and its many variations (page 98) for example. They can also add a welcome dimension to fruity and fun drinks, like in the Artichoke Hold (page 168).

Many drinks will contain both sour and bitter (and are arguably better for it) but either will refresh your mouth in readiness for the next sip!

19

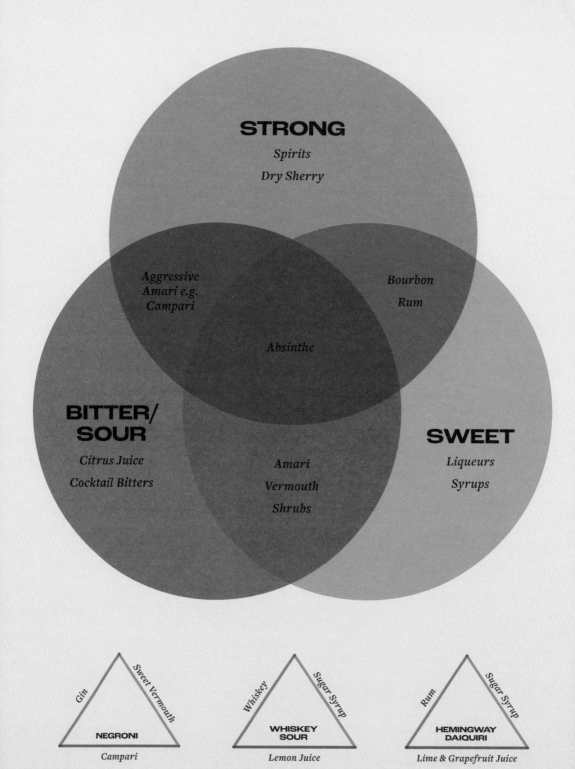

STRONG

Spirits

Dry Sherry

*Aggressive
Amari e.g.
Campari*

Bourbon

Rum

Absinthe

**BITTER/
SOUR**

Citrus Juice

Cocktail Bitters

Amari

Vermouth

Shrubs

SWEET

Liqueurs

Syrups

Gin   *Sweet Vermouth*

NEGRONI

Campari

Whiskey   *Sugar Syrup*

**WHISKEY
SOUR**

Lemon Juice

Rum   *Sugar Syrup*

**HEMINGWAY
DAIQUIRI**

Lime & Grapefruit Juice

PUT THE TASTE TRIANGLE TO THE TEST

Okay great, so all good cocktails contain strong, sweet and sour or bitter, but I promised you a practical guide, so what does that actually mean for your drink-mixing endeavours? It means that you should never not be able to make a cocktail again!

Run out of rye but you have some rum kicking around? No problem. Orange liqueur eighty-sixed but you do have some apricot brandy? Sweet as (pun intended).

Most cocktails have variations that simply switch out one ingredient for another on the same side of the triangle. Let's use the Margarita as an example:

Margarita (tequila, lime, orange liqueur)

Switch out sweet = Toreador (tequila, lime, apricot brandy) OR Tommy's Margarita (tequila, lime, agave)

Switch out strong = Pegu Club (gin, lime, orange liqueur, bitters) OR Cosmopolitan (vodka, lime, orange liqueur, cranberry juice)

Switch out sour = a Margarita made with lemon is also delicious!

You can do this deliberately to experiment with fresh takes on some of your favourites, but you can also do it on the fly – if you're missing a specific ingredient for a recipe, think about what else you have kicking around that could fulfil the same role in the Taste Triangle. This could be something else from your bar, certainly, but it could also be something in your kitchen – ripe berries or honey are excellent sweeteners, and vinegars can be used to great effect to add acid. It also means you don't have to worry about having a bottle of every spirit in your bar, which can get very expensive very quickly. You can choose a couple of your favourites and still enjoy an abundance of different drinks by switching them into recipes that call for a different base.

The Taste Triangle helps lower the barrier to entry for cocktail making – even for the disorganised among us – because you never know when the mood for a mixed drink will strike you!

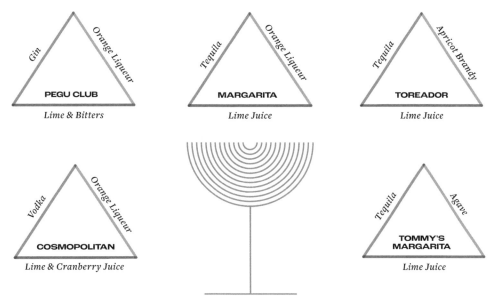

PEGU CLUB — Gin, Orange Liqueur, Lime & Bitters

MARGARITA — Tequila, Orange Liqueur, Lime Juice

TOREADOR — Tequila, Apricot Brandy, Lime Juice

COSMOPOLITAN — Vodka, Orange Liqueur, Lime & Cranberry Juice

TOMMY'S MARGARITA — Tequila, Agave, Lime Juice

HOW TO TWEAK DRINKS USING THE TASTE TRIANGLE

There's no special trick to using the Taste Triangle, but you do need to taste your drinks and – importantly – train and learn to trust your palate!

Of course everyone's tastebuds are a little different, and indeed one of the nice things about making your own drinks is that you can tailor it to your own preferences. That's totally fine – as I said, the triangle can be skewed in one direction or another, as long as all the sides are there. So if you have a sweet tooth, live your best life and add that extra bar spoon of syrup! However, if you are making drinks for other people, especially if those people are paying for them, you need to find the moreish middle ground.

Training your palate is like any other form of training – it takes practice! Yes, this is a valid excuse to drink lots of cocktails. Go to bars that use good-quality, fresh ingredients and have well-trained bartenders. Sip on your drinks slowly and really think about how the flavours are coming together in your mouth. You can do it with other things too – wine is an obvious example, but coffee or even salad dressings are a balancing act as well. You are looking for a harmony of flavours, and it will soon become obvious to you when something is out of tune.

Cocktail recipes should be seen as a jumping-off point. Unless you are using the exact same brand of products, citrus of the exact same ripeness, ice of the exact same size and so on, tweaks will have to be made to achieve that perfect harmony. Every drink should be tasted before being served, even if it's something you've made a hundred times before.

So, what to do if disaster strikes – when you taste your drink, and it's 'too' something, with one aspect sticking out incongruously?

The obvious answer is to add more of whatever ingredient is counteracting the thing that is out of balance, i.e., more sweetener if it is too sour or bitter, or vice versa. That is absolutely your first port of call – an extra bar spoon of something often works wonders – but consider your building blocks of flavour as well. Adding a large additional amount of a single ingredient will end up with that flavour overpowering everything else.

Instead, think about introducing another complementary element from the same side of the Taste Triangle.

22

How to Taste Test a Cocktail

If you're trying something new, it can be wise to taste the drink once you've combined all your ingredients, but before ice is added. This gives you more time for adjustments without it overdiluting. It will obviously be too strong at this point, but you can check all of the other elements are in balance. If it's a drink you're quite used to, a quick check after dilution will suffice to pick up any glaring issues.

The easiest way to taste a drink is using a straw (preferably a metal one to keep the turtles happy!). A spoon can work as well, but it can be a bit fiddly and you run the risk of picking up chunks of ice. Insert your straw into the liquid and place a finger over the top opening – this will create a vacuum, holding the liquid inside the straw until you put it in your mouth and remove your finger. Allow the sample to cover your tongue, and see if it tastes the way it should!

Too Strong?

Extra dilution is often all that's needed – try to do this by mixing on ice rather than just adding water as the chill factor is also important for making a cocktail slide down more smoothly. That said, not enough sweetness can also make a drink taste too sharp or boozy – sugar rounds off the rough edges, especially if your base is spicy like rye whisk(e)y or some scotches.

Too Sweet?

Try combining the forces of sour and bitter. If your main balancing ingredient is citrus but you don't want the cocktail to end up too lemony, try a dash or two of cocktail bitters to dry it out instead. Soda water (club soda), tonic water or sparkling wine also work well – lengthening out a drink decreases the perception of sweetness, with the added bonus of introducing extra bitterness (tonic) or acid (wine).

Too Bitter?

What starts off as woody intrigue in a drink can easily tip into unpleasant astringency with an overzealous helping from the bitter side of the triangle. First of all, make sure your 'strong' base can handle your bitter ingredient; rounder spirits like rum and bourbon, for instance, will stand up better to intense bitter notes than something more neutral like vodka. A little sugar also goes a long way; a bar spoon amount will often be enough to pull a rogue bitter ingredient into line without making the cocktail 'sweet'. While not part of the Taste Triangle per se, salt can also help – a pinch or a drop of saline solution knocks off the rough edges.

It's good to bear in mind that bitterness is something that people perceive differently, both on a biological level and depending on where they are in their palate journey. Many bitter drinks are also quite strong, so lengthening them out can make them more approachable – trying Campari in a spritzy Americano rather than in a Negroni, for example.

Too Sour?

Look to the sweet side. However, syrups and liqueurs can easily dominate with their pronounced flavours. Sometimes simple is best – just use sugar syrup! Or fruit juices can add a soft sweetness that is less intense and viscous – for instance if the recipe calls for elderflower liqueur and you need more sweetness but don't want it to end up too floral, apple juice is a good option.

So now we have our fundamental structure, the Taste Triangle, in place, let's get creative!

CHAPTER TWO

COCKTAIL INGREDIENTS AND HOW TO USE THEM

FLAVOUR BUILDING BLOCKS

It's important to
be aware of your
own biases, but
I swear there's
hardly a cocktail
out there that can't
be improved with a
splash of sherry.

Now that we understand the interplay of tastes integral to all good cocktails, it's time to have some fun! What base are we going to use and how are we going to layer other flavours on top, ensuring balance but also creating that wonderful alchemy that makes a drink more than the sum of its parts?

Have you ever sat in the early evening sun after a long day, taken a sip of a G&T and thought 'this is literally the best thing I've ever tasted'? Sure, some of that sentiment is situational but there's also a scientific aspect to it. The molecules in gin and tonic water are naturally attracted to each other; they form 'aggregates', new molecules that taste completely different from their constituent parts. Add a slice of lemon to highlight the limonene compound present in gin's juniper, and you have actual liquid magic. This is one of the more simple examples of how well-matched flavours can elevate your drinking to a sublime experience.

We often think of cocktail ingredients in purely alcoholic terms, and of course that's important! But flavour can also be incorporated by the use of fresh herbs, syrups, fruit, spices . . . it's really not that dissimilar to cooking!

One of my most memorable cocktails was built around a snow pea (mangetout)–infused riesling. While not the most obvious cocktail ingredient, the sweet, vegetal note of the peas played perfectly alongside the bright, bracing acidity of the wine, creating a flavour I just couldn't get enough of. That combination inspired a cocktail of mine, a snow pea–tinged Daiquiri variation I call the Tendril Lovin' (page 201) – the acid of the lime juice and juicy fruit of the white rum create a similar effect to the original, but I also layered in falernum syrup (which contains almonds) because peas and almonds share some compounds, making them molecular mates, and it really tied the whole thing together – if I do say so myself!

In this chapter we'll look at categories of spirits and alcoholic 'modifiers', but also what I like to call the 'flavour makers' – non-alcoholic ingredients that can often be made at home or in the bar – and help pack a ton of complexity and interest into your cocktail creations.

SPIRITS

Spirits have to be distilled, a process that separates the alcohol from water and other substances and then condenses it, so they sit at a higher ABV (alcohol by volume) than drinks like beer and wine, which are just fermented. Spirits also have little to no sugar added. Beyond this basic definition, the term 'spirit' is a very broad church covering everything from vodka to brandy to mezcal to baijiu. There are a few factors, though, which will always have an impact on the flavour of the finished product:

1. *What is it made from?* The primary ingredient (i.e. the fruit, grain or other plant), which is first fermented and then distilled, will have a major impact on the final flavour profile as some of its characteristics are retained – and it is often used to categorise the type of liquor produced, e.g., malt whisk(e)y must be made from malted barley.

2. *How has it been distilled?* The type, size and shape of the stills used affects which flavour compounds survive the distillation, as well as the texture of the spirit. Other parts of the production process matter as well, for example whether the barley malt is dried over peat or not in single malts. (See page 33 for more information on stills).

3. *Has it been aged?* Whether or not a spirit is aged, for how long and in what (i.e. stainless steel or barrels, and whether those barrels have previously held anything else) has a major influence on the spirit – the same spirit can taste and feel entirely different at various stages of the ageing process.

4. *Has anything been added?* Botanicals and flavourings (rather than the base spirit/wine) make up the flavour profiles of key categories like gin, amari, spiced rum etc. Because of this, these can be the easiest ones to hone your palate on as the flavours are more identifiable.

Taking note of these factors for every spirit you try can help you start to navigate through your likes and dislikes, or what works well in certain drinks.

28

What Do We Mean by Flavours in Spirits?

Some alcohols have flavours added, which makes pulling out flavours quite straightforward. A spiced rum, for example, could have notes of vanilla, cinnamon and orange and that will be because the base spirit has been infused with them. But even spirits with nothing added will have identifiable flavours and aromas. Smelling is so important when getting to know spirits, but keep your mouth open and don't stick your nose too far in the glass or you'll burn your nose hairs off!

Fermentation and distillation form flavour compounds that can also be found in fruits, herbs and vegetables. So an unspiced rum can taste like tropical fruit (bananas and pineapples) with no fruit having been harmed in its production at all! Wood-ageing also brings in lots more flavours. American oak is known for the vanilla flavour that makes bourbon taste like bourbon, for example. All spirits are technically dry – their sugars have been converted to alcohol. That said, some will have a perception of sweetness because of sweeter flavour compounds, or a perception of dryness because of woodier flavours, and it's good to bear this in mind when balancing your drinks.

These flavours can be trickier to pick out – you do have to practise, but they're in there, I promise! Don't be afraid to add a little water if it helps you see past the alcohol burn and taste widely (both alcohol and the real deal: fruits, herbs and so on) so you start to build up a sense memory and are able to recognise flavours more easily.

● VODKA

Is Vodka Gluten-free?

All spirits are gluten-free, despite attempts by some marketing executives to convince us otherwise – the gluten proteins don't survive the distilling process. Shots all round!

The much-maligned antihero of the late 20th century, I think vodka gets a bad rap. It is intentionally made to be a clean spirit and as such makes an excellent base to carry other flavours. Not all spirits have to have main-character syndrome! Because it is an unaged spirit, and the vast majority of vodka is distilled on the same kind of still (a column still – see page 33), its personality will mostly be formed by what it is made from – wheat, rye, grape, even potato. This is definitely a category where you should be wary of spending too much, as often the extra money spent on 'premium' vodka goes to marketing rather than quality! As long as the spirit is not unpleasantly rough and hot it will work well in most drinks. Look for a nice oily, viscous texture when using it in more spirit-forward cocktails like a Vodka Martini (aka Kangaroo).

Usually tastes like: citrus, peppery spice, cream
Pairs well with: berry fruit, citrus, herbal

● GIN

This may strike a dagger in the hearts of some, but gin is, essentially, flavoured vodka. Evolving from the Dutch spirit genever, modern gin is a neutral spirit base flavoured with botanicals, one of which has to be juniper to give it its distinctive character. Old Tom–style gins lean to the sweeter side, either with sweetener added or by using sweeter botanicals, but the London Dry style became much more prevalent in the 20th century and is the most common one drunk today. While each distillery decides their own proprietary botanical blend, anything labelled 'London Dry' sticks to a 'classic' gin profile with piney juniper very much at the forefront, supported by citrus notes and woody spices (and they don't actually have to come from London). This style works well in the majority of gin cocktails.

Stone fruit:
apricot, nectarine, peach

Orchard fruit:
apple, pear

That said, gin is having a bit of a moment and the explosion of new distilleries has seen all sorts of weird and wonderful flora and fauna being chucked in the distillation pot – producers are more often looking to indigenous ingredients to give their spirit a personality reflective of its surroundings (think seaweed in Ireland, green tea in Japan and green ants in Australia!). While this means that not every bottle of gin you pick up will work equally well in every cocktail, it does leave plenty of room for experimentation. Because the actual plants are used in the distillation process, it can be easier to pick out individual flavours and aromas in gin than in other spirits, and so is a good place to start some flavour-pairing practice, even if it's just with an interesting tonic water and fragrant garnish.

Usually tastes like: citrus, woody spice, floral
Pairs well with: stone fruit, berry fruit, herbal

● AGAVE SPIRITS – TEQUILA

All tequila is mezcal but not all mezcal is tequila. Both are made in Mexico from agave plants (which are actually not cacti, contrary to common belief – good pub trivia question there!). For the spirit to be labelled tequila it has to meet strict criteria including being made only in certain regions, primarily the town of Tequila in Jalisco, and from blue agave specifically, the hearts (or piñas) of which are steamed or roasted before distillation. Where the agave is grown has a big effect on the flavour of the spirit (terroir isn't just for wine!) but a grassy, savoury and herbal spirit with a hint of tropical fruit sweetness is to be expected.

It is delicious unaged (blanco) and aged (reposado, añejo or extra añejo). Time in barrel adds depth and warm notes of baking spices and caramel to the bright, fresh unaged spirit; all iterations can be used to excellent effect in cocktails.

Tequila doesn't have to be 100% agave and those that aren't (mixto) are probably the ones that gave you a hangover in university – don't hold it against the whole category! Also, agave farmers have experienced mounting pressure as demand for tequila grows so some producers are taking shortcuts, which affects not only the quality of the spirit but also the environment. Basically, if a bottle of tequila is cheap . . . don't buy it.

Usually tastes like: peppery spice, floral, grassy (+ baking spice and vanilla when aged)
Pairs well with: citrus, stone fruit, chilli spice

● AGAVE SPIRITS – MEZCAL

Mezcal is made elsewhere in Mexico (primarily Oaxaca) and from a variety of agaves (the most common being espadin, but plenty of others are used), which has a big impact on flavour. It can also be aged or unaged. The traditional method is to bake the agave hearts underground with wood charcoal (rather than steaming or roasting) and this imparts a distinctive smoky flavour. With lots of variables and much less regulation than tequila it is a rather diverse spirit – it can range from floral and citrus-driven with just a hint of smoke, to the sort of smoky intensity rarely seen outside of Islay scotch! In fact in my house, we drink whisk(e)y in winter and mezcal in summer; both are excellent sipping spirits and mezcal has a freshness perfect for hot days. It is a complex and intriguing spirit that, again, tends to come with a higher price tag due to the artisanal methods of production.

Usually tastes like: earthy, smoky, peppery spice (+ baking spice and vanilla when aged)
Pairs well with: citrus, tropical fruit, baking spice

31

● RUM

Rum is, quite literally, a sticky subject. It is a distilled spirit made from sugarcane, but that's about all anyone can agree on. There are many countries with their own proud tradition, and definition, of what we call rum (and some that we don't even call rum, like cachaça!). Above all, don't rely on colour alone – white rum can be aged and filtered, and dark or 'gold' rum can have colouring added.

Historically, rum was broken down according to the colonial powers' distilling traditions – English, French, Spanish and Portuguese. But there has been a move away from using this language because, a) we need to stop glorifying that sh*t and, b) it's actually just not that useful any more as distilleries diversify production. Instead, it's much more useful to fall back on asking: what's it made from, how is it made and is it aged?

Rum can be made from freshly-pressed sugarcane juice or molasses (a syrupy by-product of sugar production). As you can imagine, rums made from the former are fresher and grassier, and rums made from the latter are more intensely flavoured and fruitier. Molasses-based rum makes up the majority of what we know as rum – rhum agricole and cachaça are delicious outliers made from the fresh juice.

Then we have the production method – pot still rums will be heavier and funkier, column still rums lighter in body, and you can also get blends of both. Ageing has the same effect on rum as it does on all spirits, rounding them out and adding sweetness and spice. So, the same cocktail made with a column-distilled, unaged rum will be entirely different from one made with a pot-distilled, aged rum, but there will be some shared flavour notes if they're both made from molasses. Try both in a Daiquiri and you'll quickly understand – it's for research purposes *wink*.

Usually tastes like: tropical fruit, baking spice, caramel sweetness
Pairs well with: citrus, tropical fruit, bitter

What Does the Still Have to Do with It?

The still is where the magic happens. It is the device by which spirits are made – alcoholic liquid (a ferment) is heated to create a vapour and then condensed back into liquid again, but much of the water has evaporated, leaving you with a higher ABV liquid – forget water into wine, this is wine into brandy! The shape and style of the still will have a major impact on the flavour of the final spirit – in fact, many distilleries will dent and bash new stills in the exact same places as their old ones for fear of losing any of the unique character of their spirit. There are essentially two kinds of still – the pot still and the column still.

The pot still is the OG, also known as an alembic still, invented back in the 8th century by an Arab alchemist named Abū Mūsā Jābir ibn Hayyān – cheers pal! It still really hasn't changed much since then and is essentially a kettle, almost always made of copper, where the spirit is distilled in batches. Pot stills produce heavier, more flavourful distillates.

The column, or continuous, still was invented in the early 19th century by a Scotsman named Robert Stein, then refined by an Irishman named Aeneas Coffey, which is why it is sometimes known as a Coffey still. It is much larger than a pot still and can be copper, stainless steel or a mix of both. It essentially works like a series of pot stills stacked on top of each other, and runs continuously, rather than in batches. It can produce a much higher volume and distil to a much higher ABV, making it very useful for the mass production of spirits. It produces lighter, more neutral distillates.

Both types of still are used across basically all spirits categories, but the difference is well illustrated in rum, where pot stills produce powerful, funky expressions and column stills produce more delicate, fruity and herbal expressions.

● BRANDY

Brandy is another extremely diverse category, both stylistically and geographically. It is basically any spirit that is made from distilling fermented fruit juice. It is generally understood that if something is just called 'brandy' it will have been made from grapes but you can also get, for example, apple or pear brandy – it's a logical by-product of fruit-growing. The quality varies wildly from low-grade cooking brandy through to some of the most elite spirits in the world. Particular regions that are well known for brandy will have tighter regulations around what can have their name on the label, hence why places such as Cognac, Armagnac and Jerez are seen as benchmarks. I once knew a man who bought himself a bottle of Armagnac from his birth year every birthday – I often wonder if he's still able to continue the tradition or if he's got all the ones that haven't been drunk by now! He was generous enough to share them around, and tasting a 1960s Armagnac was a truly formative experience in appreciating the alchemy of a well-made spirit.

Unaged brandy generally goes by its own name depending on where it is made (eau-de-vie, grappa, pisco etc.). If something is just labelled 'brandy' it is assumed it has seen some time in oak – adding spice, sweetness and tannin to the fresh flavours of the distillate – but they tend to retain a juicy fruit character, which is very moreish.

Brandy was once as popular as whisk(e)y for use in cocktails, if not more so, but a root disease called phylloxera decimated the French wine industry in the mid-19th century. It took a while for stocks to build back up and brandy to be readily available again, by which point other spirits had a firm grip on the market. With the digging up of historical cocktail recipes, a new generation of bartenders fell in love with brandy and it can be used to great effect in a plethora of cocktail styles.

Usually tastes like: dried fruit, baking spice, woody spice
Pairs well with: citrus, cream, stone fruit

⚫⚫ WHISK(E)Y – BOURBON

From the laissez-faire approach of rum and brandy to one of the most well-regulated spirits in the world, bourbon must be made from at least 51% corn (but not more than 79%) and aged in new charred-oak barrels (for at least two years to have the word 'straight' on the label, and if less than four years, the age must also be displayed). This ageing process imparts the characteristic toasty and vanilla notes we know and love. Think of cornbread – bourbon is on the sweeter side, with a rich and bold flavour. Brands are mostly differentiated by their 'mash bill', i.e., what other grains are in the mix with the corn, and how much of each. A bourbon with more wheat will be sweeter and softer; one with a high rye content will be spicier and dryer. Bourbon is not just for shots in dive bars (although it's great for that too!); there are some ambrosial sippers out there too.

It is the United States' national spirit – while corn whisk(e)y can certainly be made elsewhere, to be called bourbon it has to be made in the US and, unsurprisingly, given the strong cocktail culture there, it is an exceptionally versatile cocktail ingredient.

Usually tastes like: caramel sweetness, baking spice, vanilla
Pairs well with: citrus, bitter, stone fruit

⚫ WHISK(E)Y – RYE

The US may be the first country that comes to mind when thinking about rye whisk(e)y but it is made in other countries too, notably Canada and Australia. In the US, rye has similar rules to bourbon – it must be at least 51% rye grain and aged in new charred oak barrels (for at least two years to have the word 'straight' on the label, and if less than four years the age must also be displayed). Rye differs, though, in that it can be up to 100% rye grain. Other countries have more lenient rules, but all rye whisk(e)y has a characteristic pepperiness and grassiness – again, think of rye bread, dense and spicy – it adds massive depth and complexity to mixed drinks. It's one of my favourite spirits to build a cocktail around, providing a spicy backbone that works well with the seasonal fruits and herbs I like to use.

Usually tastes like: peppery spice, grassy, earthy
Pairs well with: citrus, orchard fruit, caramel sweetness

Order Whisk(e)y How You Like It

Neat Nothing but whisk(e)y in the glass. This will usually be served in a tasting glass in more specialist venues.

On the rocks More ice actually slows the dilution – one big block of ice or a few cubes will melt more slowly than a single small cube.

Water on the side Your whisk(e)y will be served neat with a little jug of water alongside, so you can add dilution as you need for your own taste (my personal preference!).

● WHISK(E)Y – SINGLE MALT

While 'single malt' is generally thought of as a co-dependent phrase (and indeed a complete drinks order in movies, no further clarification needed – don't get me started on the unreality of that!) these two words denote two separate things. 'Single' refers to it coming from one distillery; 'malt' refers to it being 100% malted barley. Blended malts are actually reasonably common, and can be a happy medium for cocktails, having all the weight and texture of malt whisk(e)y without the (sometimes larger than life) distillery traits. But I digress.

Once upon a time, when talking of single malts we would have assumed we were based in Scotland (perhaps Ireland), but the popularity of the style has caused an explosion of distilleries and there are now single malt whiskies being made worldwide – the US, Australia, Japan, India, Taiwan – although Scotland still has the strictest rules around what can be labelled a single malt Scotch.

Not all single malts are peated but Scotland produces the majority of those that are, with Islay in particular being renowned for it. Peat is used to dry the barley during the malting process, imbuing the final spirit with a smoky, savoury earthiness, which people generally either love or hate. It can be hard to handle in cocktails as it overpowers everything else but can be used judiciously to great effect.

Another major factor in the flavour of single malts is the barrels they are aged in. Unlike with bourbon and rye, they are aged in 'refill casks' that have held something else previously – usually (but not restricted to) bourbon or a fortified wine – and take on some of the previous resident's characteristics. A single malt aged in a sherry cask, for instance, will be rich with lots of dried fruit flavours.

Given the idiosyncratic nature of single malts and the higher price tag attached to them, it is unusual for them to be called for in generic cocktail recipes but it can be fun to build bespoke cocktails around a favourite of yours!

Usually tastes like (disclaimer: as much as there are many!): dried fruit, savoury, woody spice
Pairs well with: baking spice, orchard fruit, citrus

● WHISK(E)Y – BLENDED

Not to be confused with the blended malts discussed opposite, blended whisk(e)y is a mix of malt and grain whisk(e)y. The Scots had struggled to convince others to embrace their beloved single malts, with foreigners finding them too powerful for their delicate palates. The invention of the column still (see page 33) changed this. The lighter whisk(e)y coming off this new still type could be blended with malt whisk(e)y to create a less challenging, still delicious, product. In fact, when I was a kid, blends were much more popular than single malts – my grandpa's tipple of choice (along with many of his peers) was a 'hauf 'n' hauf', a nip of blended Scotch with a half pint of Scottish lager.

The same remains true today. While whisk(e)y connoisseurs may turn their noses up at blends, they are far more consistent and therefore versatile in cocktail making. Again, they are now a worldwide phenomenon and often represent a pocket-friendly introduction to the wonderful world of whisk(e)y. Many famous blends come from Scotland but they're also common in other whisk(e)y-producing countries like Ireland, Japan and Canada.

Usually tastes like: orchard fruit, cereal grain, honey sweetness
Pairs well with: baking spice, citrus, stone fruit

ALCOHOLIC MODIFIERS

How Do I Choose What to Buy?

Stocking a bar can be overwhelming and expensive – start with just a few key bottles and build from there. In a bar environment you want to have at least one of each of the major spirits and modifier categories, but at home you can look at getting a couple of your favourite spirits and a range of modifiers (which are generally less costly) and that will allow you to continue to mix things up – literally!

When it comes to brands, you really have to make the decision according to your budget and what's important to you. Supporting local independents tends to be a little more expensive without the economies of scale, and there's more risk of inconsistent products from tiny producers; big name brands might not be the most exciting, but they are reliable and readily available. Taste as much as you can, whether in bars, doing online tastings or going old school and inviting a group of friends to all bring a bottle to a get together (but do take notes or photos – things can get a little hazy!). Start to build a picture of your likes and dislikes. Consider what kind of cocktails you're making as well. If you're going to be using lots of syrups and juices then you'll want something robust and not too nuanced as it will get lost; if it's a booze-forward cocktail then it might be time to let that special bottle shine.

This term covers the group of ingredients used in cocktails to add flavour and interest to drinks – not that spirits are boring by any stretch of the imagination, but if you only wanted to drink them neat you wouldn't be reading this book! In *The Fine Art of Mixing Drinks*, bon vivant David Embury says of 'the modifying agent' (as he calls it), 'It is this ingredient, in combination with the base of spirituous liquor, which characterizes the cocktail . . . the modifier should add that elusive je ne sais quoi which makes the cocktail a smooth, fragrant, inspirational delight and not a mere drink of gin or whisk(e)y'. While I don't agree with his assertion that these ingredients should always play second fiddle to the spirit base, their importance certainly cannot be underestimated!

●● FORTIFIED WINES – AROMATISED WINES

Unlike other fortified wines like sherry and port, which develop their flavour profile from the grapes and ageing process, aromatised wine is all about the additives. Botanicals are macerated in the base wine to create a complex and nuanced drink reflective of the landscapes they come from; they're basically a cocktail in themselves, with herbs and barks providing bitterness and fruits, florals and citrus (plus additional sugar) providing sweetness.

Vermouth is the most well-known of the aromatised wines (see below) but there are others. For instance, quinquinas have quinine as their main bittering ingredient (Lillet and Dubonnet being the most famous), and Americanos (derived from the French word amer, or bitter), such as Cocchi Americano, usually rely on gentian, but honestly it's all a little blurry and usually really just depends what the producer has decided to call the product!

Often relegated to the supporting act in cocktails, I love putting these wines centre stage for a lower ABV but unabashedly flavourful tipple.

Usually tastes like: citrus, woody spice, herbal
Pairs well with: there's a fortified wine to pair with basically everything!

●● FORTIFIED WINES – VERMOUTH

Vermouth is a subcategory of aromatised wines but, given its venerable place in the cocktail maker's arsenal, it certainly seems worthy of its own introduction. The name comes from Wermut, German for wormwood, the presence of which delineates vermouth from other aromatised wines (they have to contain it by EU law) and provides a bitter backbone. Otherwise, they are flavoured with a similar bouquet of herbs, barks and spices, with each producer having a proprietary blend – the flavour profile can vary widely even between vermouths that look a similar colour.

There are two major styles – dry and sweet (sometimes known as red vermouth). In historical cocktail recipes, dry vermouth was referred to as French and sweet as Italian, but vermouth is made all over the world now and most producers make more than one style so it's not a very useful distinction nowadays.

Solera System

Put simply, this means that barrels are topped up with newer wines as the older wines are taken out to be bottled. It is a system also common in rum production, and means that every bottling benefits from both the complexity and depth of age and the freshness of youth! It's why you'll sometimes see years like '1824' on bottles; that's when the solera was started so, while it's not all 200-year-old booze, there is a small percentage of it in there.

Even dry vermouth still has some sugar added, but significantly less than those designated 'sweet'; they are straw-coloured and their botanicals tend towards citrus, floral and herbal and so they play nicely with lighter spirits. Sweet vermouth tends more towards dark fruits (mirrored in their reddish-brown colour), woody spices and caramel, so they stand up nicely to darker spirits. There is also a middle ground which I'm quite a fan of – the blanco/blanc/bianco vermouth, which is also straw-coloured and citrus-driven but contains more sugar than dry vermouth, giving it more weight and presence in cocktails.

Usually tastes like: citrus, woody spice, herbal
Pairs well with: there's a vermouth to pair with basically everything!

● FORTIFIED WINES – DRY SHERRY

It's important to be aware of your own biases, but I swear there's hardly a cocktail out there that can't be improved with a splash of sherry – stick some manzanilla in your Bloody Mary and thank me later *wink*. This is not your nana's sherry though. For a long time, sherry was synonymous with sticky sweet cream and Pedro Ximénez (PX) wines, but actually the majority of sherry is dry. It ranges from delicate, floral and steely manzanilla and fino, through to nutty amontillado to rich and dried fruit–driven oloroso, all made from the same palomino grape. The key to this wonderful range is 'flor', a layer of yeast that grows over the wine and protects more delicate wines from the air; or is killed off and oxygen allowed in to add richness. The solera ageing system also adds complexity and depth and this means these wines are more than capable of underpinning a cocktail as the 'strong' element as well as being useful modifiers.

Usually tastes like: nutty, herbal, savoury (+ dried fruit in amontillado and oloroso)
Pairs well with: woody spice, citrus, stone fruit

● FORTIFIED WINES – SWEET SHERRY/PORT/MADEIRA

It's perhaps unfair to bundle all these esteemed wines together but they perform a very similar task in cocktails – adding roundness and richness. Good-quality versions of these wines get their sweetness from using late-harvest or dried grapes, which have a higher sugar content, and having their fermentation stopped before all of the sugar is fermented to alcohol (leaving what is known as 'residual sugar' in the wines). Some will be lighter in body and drier, such as Sercial Madeira, and some will be like liquid treacle (looking at you, PX), but they all add sweetness to drinks in a sophisticated and interesting way.

Usually tastes like: dried fruit, nutty, caramel sweetness
Pairs well with: baking spice, citrus, bitter

⬤⬤ AMARI

'Amaro' means bitter in Italian, and covers the incredibly wide category of bitter herbal liqueurs made by steeping botanicals in spirits or wine, and adding sugar. There are massive regional and stylistic variations, from red citrus-driven ones like Campari, to dark and brooding ones like the Fernet family of amari. They do all have sugar added as well in varying quantities, so can add a viscosity to drinks and balance themselves somewhat.

Whereas vermouth is defined by wormwood as the bittering agent, amari can be bittered by any number of things – wormwood too, but also gentian, cinchona and even rhubarb. And, whereas vermouth is always wine-based, amari are more often based on a distilled spirit, such as brandy. That said, amari can be wine-based and there's definitely a bit of a blurred line between the two, a more pronounced bitterness being the hallmark of an amaro, but also conversely more sugar added, which doesn't make them sweet but gives a richer texture.

Aside from actual cocktail bitters, they are the most common way to introduce a beguiling bitter edge to your drinks, which is often what adds sophistication to mixed drinks. They're also somewhat of a bartender's handshake – if someone orders a shot of chilled Fernet-Branca in your bar they're almost certainly in the trade! My personal favourite is a Rum Monty – a shot of half rum and half Montenegro.

Usually tastes like: bitter, woody spice, herbal
Pairs well with: all fruits, caramel sweetness, cereal grain

⬤ COCKTAIL BITTERS

There's often a je ne sais quoi about drinking a cocktail in a bar as opposed to at home, and while it's probably partly just because someone else is making it for you (and washing up afterwards!), another educated guess would be that they've added some bitters.

Bitters are made by infusing aromatics, such as fruit and barks, in neutral alcohol to produce a really strong flavouring (they are usually only administered as drops or dashes). They were originally marketed for medicinal purposes and so traditional bitters contain lots of barks and herbs with alleged curative properties; they could almost be described as concentrated, unsweetened versions of amari. They made the jump to the bar, and since bartenders love their flavour-enhancing properties, many that are specifcally tailored to cocktail making have also hit the market with weird and wonderful flavourings.

While lots of cocktails actually call for bitters, there aren't that many more that don't still benefit from a dash or two. Bitters add depth and length to a cocktail. They help the flavours from other ingredients linger, and that's what makes an unforgettable cocktail.

Usually tastes like: bitter, woody spice, herbal
Pairs well with: there's a cocktail bitters to pair with basically everything!

●●● ABSINTHE

Absinthe is technically a spirit, but its strong flavour profile means that it is more often used in small amounts as a modifier. It is made in much the same way as gin, by macerating botanicals in a neutral spirit. The hallmarks of absinthe are the use of wormwood, and a distinctive aniseed taste coming from ingredients like liquorice, star anise and sweet fennel (which also provide a naturally sweet counterbalance to wormwood's bitterness).

Hysteria over the supposed hallucinogenic effects of absinthe meant that there were widespread bans on it for quite a while, and so a few products entered the market to fill the gap with a similar flavour profile, but are sweeter and lower in alcohol (technically liqueurs): pastis and Herbsaint. Both can easily replace absinthe in a cocktail recipe that only calls for a few dashes; in fact, their softer feel often makes them easier to work with.

Usually tastes like: herbal, woody spice, bittersweet
Pairs well with: orchard fruit, stone fruit, citrus

● LIQUEURS

The first thing that jumps to mind upon hearing the word liqueur may well be rows of tacky bottles, all in improbable luminescent colours and indistinctly sweet. It is true that such sticky concoctions, which bear nothing but a passing resemblance to the organic flavour on their label, come under the umbrella of liqueur, but so do herbal and intricate brews like Chartreuse and Benedictine, delicate and floral delights like St Germain, and zesty zingers like a well-made curaçao. Liqueurs use spirits as a base and are sweetened and flavoured – beyond that, it's a free for all.

While generally less expensive than good-quality spirits, it is still worth spending a little more than the bare minimum on your liqueurs to ensure they are not completely artificial and sickly sweet.

This is definitely a category where personal preference comes in when stocking a home bar – if you're not a big fan of orange liqueurs, for example, you can easily buy a bottle of apricot brandy or elderflower liqueur and use that instead. Similarly, in a bar environment, you don't really have to have every single berry liqueur on your back bar – crème de mûre, crème de cassis and so on can usually be used pretty interchangeably.

Usually tastes like: sweet, fruity, floral
Pairs well with: bitter, spice, herbal

Triple Sec versus Curaçao

There is actually no legal difference between these two names for orange liqueur – brands can just choose what they want to be known as. Curaçao is named after the island but doesn't have to be made there. A rash of not very good curaçaos caused some well-respected brands to move away from the name, most of which were French – 'triple sec' indicated that you could expect the product to be drier, but there are also some great dry curaçaos out there too. Orange liqueurs based on brandy like Grand Marnier will be rounder and richer; ones based on neutral spirits, such as Cointreau, will be brighter and fresher. You can absolutely substitute them, but it will affect the flavour of the drink.

How Should I Store My Booze?

Spirits are very stable due to their alcohol content. Try to store out of direct sunlight and they will be fine for years (although if you only have a little left in a bottle, then it's better just to finish it off than keep it for too long – it loses potency). It follows that things based on spirits (like most liqueurs and amari) are also stable, and need not be refrigerated.

Anything wine-based, though, should be refrigerated. The wine base oxidises in the same way regular wine does, just more slowly due to the extra fortification. The more delicate the flavour the more obvious it will be – dry vermouths and fino and manzanilla sherries will start to fall over after a couple of weeks in the fridge; dry but oxidised wines like amontillado and oloroso will last about a month; and sweetened fortified wines can last up to a year. Note that I say 'fall over', not 'go off' – nothing will be wrong with them per se, but they will lose intensity of aroma and eventually start to taste raisiny or even vinegary.

THE FLAVOUR MAKERS

The alcoholic ingredients often hog the limelight but, for true versatility, seasonality and, let's be honest, thriftiness, homemade ingredients are your friend! Based on ancient preservation methods, they're a great way to use up surplus fruit, and by making them yourself you can control sweetness and layer in other flavours through spices and herbs.

● SYRUPS AND CORDIALS

A thick, sweet liquid made by dissolving sugar in water, syrups are an easy way to introduce the requisite sweetness to your drinks. Cordials are another version of this – they used to contain alcohol but nowadays usually don't and are often based on fruit juice, while syrups are sugar and water. Regular sugar syrup is a staple of cocktail making, but one of the easiest ways to zhuzh your drink is to flavour it. The simplest method is just to steep your desired flavour in syrup overnight (or heat gently on the stove to expedite the process) – try different teas, peppercorns, mint or vanilla pods. You can also make flavoured syrups by combining fruit and sugar. Doing this yourself allows you to layer in other flavours and tailor it specifically to the cocktail you have in mind. You can always scale any recipe to the amount of drinks you need to make as well.

44

How Simple is Simple Sugar Syrup?

Answer: very! Please never spend money on store-bought sugar syrup. It is literally just sugar and water, combined in equal parts. You can use hot water, heat very gently on the stove, or just stir furiously until the sugar is dissolved and voila! It's much easier to work with a liquid in cocktails so definitely worth the couple of minutes it takes to make, rather than struggling with granulated sugar.

Occasionally recipes will call for a 'rich' sugar syrup, which is 2 parts sugar to 1 part water for a more concentrated sweetness. Regular sugar syrup is made with fine white sugar (not icing/confectioners' sugar), but you can also use things like demerara or muscovado for a more caramelised flavour, which works well with darker spirits.

SPICED BERRY SYRUP

This is such an easy one and can be substituted into cocktails that call for grenadine or raspberry syrup, but also has enough going on that it can be used with just some lemon juice and soda water (club soda) – and gin if you feel like it! Of course, if berries are in season then use fresh, but otherwise frozen packs work really well and you can always have them on hand. You can use whichever spices you like, and feel free to adjust the sweetness to your own palate.

INGREDIENTS

500 g (1 lb 2 oz) mixed berries

250 g (9 oz) granulated white sugar

250 ml (1 cup) water

2 strips lemon peel

1 cinnamon stick

6 cloves

2 cardamom pods

EQUIPMENT

Saucepan

Spoon

Strainer

METHOD

Place all the ingredients in a saucepan and heat gently until combined. Reduce to a syrupy consistency – it will thicken as it cools, but it should still be pourable and you want to retain a fresh flavour, so don't take it too far. Strain and use as you like! Keep in an airtight container in the fridge for 1–2 weeks, but it can also be frozen for up to 3 months.

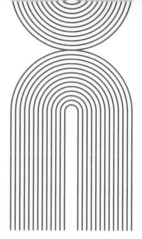

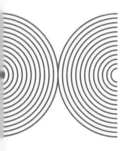

Some syrups that crop up time and again in cocktail making are grenadine, falernum syrup and orgeat. Good-quality commercial versions can be found nowadays, and are useful if you only make drinks sporadically, as they are more shelf stable. To be honest, I find falernum syrup and orgeat a bit of a faff – they're quite involved recipes (although you can find some good hacks online), so I tend to stick to store-bought ones unless making them the hero of the drink. Grenadine, though, is very easy and making it at home ensures the lip-smacking tartness of the pomegranate is retained.

GRENADINE

This same method can be applied to other fruit juices and complementary flavours – apple juice seasoned with cinnamon and clove for instance, or watermelon juice with mint.

INGREDIENTS

500 ml (2 cups) pomegranate juice

500 g (1 lb 2 oz) granulated white sugar

60 ml (¼ cup) pomegranate molasses

5 ml (⅙ fl oz) orange blossom water

2 strips lemon zest

EQUIPMENT

Saucepan

Spoon

Strainer

METHOD

Place all the ingredients in a saucepan and heat gently until combined. Reduce to a syrupy consistency – it will thicken as it cools, but it should still be pourable and you want to retain a fresh flavour, so don't take it too far. Strain and use as you like! Keep in an airtight container in the fridge for 1–2 weeks, but it can also be frozen for up to 3 months.

⬤⬤ OLEO SACCHARUM

It may sound like a bit of a mouthful but don't be scared; this ingredient is nowhere near as complicated as it sounds and has been used in drinks since the first Punch recipes started floating around in the 1600s – before cocktails were even a twinkle in the eye! The literal meaning is 'oil sugar', and the idea is that rough sugar can extract all the flavourful oils from citrus skins, giving a perfumed and delicious 'oil' to use in drinks. There are a few advantages to this. One is that since so much citrus juice is used in cocktails, this is an awesome way to make sure you're getting full use of your lemons by using the zest as well! Another is that, since no heat is applied in the process, the end flavour is as fresh and zingy as you could hope and brings a citrus sourness to drinks and, because no water is added, it is a very concentrated flavour. This is why it works so well in Punch-style drinks as it doesn't get lost when they are lengthened out with water or juice. As Jerry Thomas said in his 1862 book *The Bartenders Guide*, 'to make punch of any sort in perfection, the ambrosial essence of the lemon must be extracted', and luckily a new generation of bartenders are coming back round to this way of thinking!

CITRUS OLEO

This is a citrus syrup recipe that is infinitely adaptable to whatever citrus and spices you have around – grapefruits, oranges and lemons all work really well, and I've made a mandarin one before, which was delicious with tequila! In a bar environment it's really helpful if you have a vacuum pack machine – you can do larger quantities and seal it in to do its thing overnight with minimal effort. It still definitely works at home, but leave it covered at room temperature, rather than in the fridge, and give it a good pound with a muddler or similar to start off and stir a few times when you remember!

INGREDIENTS

Peel of 1 grapefruit

Peel of 1 orange

Peel of 3 lemons

Granulated white sugar to cover

Pink peppercorns (or other spices – experiment – clove also works well!)

EQUIPMENT

Vegetable peeler

Muddler

Bowl

Strainer

METHOD

Remove any excess white pith from the peel. Place in a bowl and cover with the sugar and peppercorns or other spices. Pound with a muddler, cover and leave for at least a few hours (but preferably overnight), stirring occasionally. Strain out the peel and enjoy! For a delicious homemade sour mix, simply dissolve the oleo syrup in citrus juice.

◐● SHRUBS

There are two types of shrubs, one of which is similar to a Punch and includes alcohol, but more commonly nowadays we are talking about the sweetened, vinegar-based syrup version. Shrubs are proof that not all cocktail fads should be dismissed – they exploded back onto the scene a couple of years ago but have proven their staying power because of their vinegar backbone. This means that as much as they are a sweet component, they also BYO acid – a balanced ingredient in its own right is every bartender's dream, and ideal if you don't always have access to fresh citrus. Both types of shrubs evolved from 'sherbets', a drink with roots in Persia, Turkey and surrounding areas. These are also an easy and delicious non-alcoholic option just lengthened out with soda water (club soda).

These basic methods can be applied across any number of fruits (or even vegetables – try a rhubarb syrup or beetroot/beet shrub!) with different spice or herb accents. Having a few 'flavour maker' ingredients in your repertoire, and an eye on flavour pairing, can help you make boundless twists on classics or build entirely new creations based on whatever caught your eye at the market this week – and without having to invest in another bottle!

PINEAPPLE SHRUB

This recipe almost starts out life as an oleo – pineapple gives off lots of juice when covered in sugar and creates its own syrup. Again, the spices are optional and totally up to your own tastes – feel free to experiment. If you can find a vinegar to complement the flavours you're after that's ideal, otherwise apple cider vinegar or white wine vinegar are good choices as they are fruity and still quite delicate.

INGREDIENTS

1 pineapple, cubed

2.5 cm (1 inch) piece of ginger, cubed

4 allspice berries

Cane sugar to cover

Around 500 ml (2 cups) pineapple vinegar

EQUIPMENT

Sterilised jar

Strainer

METHOD

Place the pineapple in a sterilised jar with the ginger and spices and cover with the sugar. Seal and leave overnight, shaking occasionally. Strain and add the 500 ml (2 cups) pineapple vinegar, or a bit more or less, to taste – it should be bright and sharp but not unpleasantly acidic.

CHAPTER THREE

TOOLS AND SETUP

BEHIND THE BAR

Do not underestimate
the importance of
having a tea towel or
cloth to hand (literally!)

Before we get to actually making drinks though, we have to set up our bar. There are, of course, gadgets and shiny things galore and I'm certainly not saying you should avoid them – bartending is partially about putting on a show, after all – but a lot of them are not necessary, especially when first setting up a bar. If budget is an issue, my advice would be to concentrate on stocking your bar with good quality booze before ostentatious bar tools. Some of the best Margaritas I've ever had were shaken up in a tupperware container!

BAR EQUIPMENT ESSENTIALS

1. JIGGER

This is probably the most important piece of equipment in a bartender's arsenal. It may look cool to free-pour (pouring alcohol without measuring it) but very few people are willing to put in the hours of practice it takes to actually get good at it! A jigger will make sure that you are turning out consistently well balanced drinks. There are different kinds and sizes depending what style of bartending you are doing. If you only have one, a classic double jigger will do the job – one end of this is a standard shot (so 30 ml, 1 oz, 25 ml depending what country you are in) and the other end is a double shot, plus there are markings on the inside for 15 ml, 20 ml (or ½ oz, ¾ oz) and so on. If you're going to be pumping out a high volume of cocktails, consider a 'graduated measure' – it is a larger measure with 'steps' of 15 ml (or ½ oz) increments, so you can build a whole cocktail in there.

2. SHAKER

The two main types of shaker are Boston and Cobbler. Most bars now use what is known as 'tin on tin' Boston shakers, which is pretty self explanatory. They are relatively inexpensive, easy to clean, big enough to build two cocktails, hard to break and if you buy the same brand for all of them you can mix and match the larger and smaller halves so you don't have to worry about losing pieces (things disappear surprisingly easily in a bar...). There are also Bostons where one half is glass – this allows you to see what you're building in there but they are heavier and more likely to break so most bars have moved away from them. The last kind are Cobblers, also known as three piece shakers. They are by far the most aesthetically pleasing kind, and have a built in strainer so can work well for home use but are smaller and harder to clean so are not as useful for high-volume bartending.

3. STRAINERS

There are three types of cocktail strainer commonly found in any bar: the Julep, the Hawthorne and the fine strainer. The Julep strainer is the oldest and simplest way of holding the ice back as you pour the drink into your glass. This one has been around basically since ice started being used in cocktails, but you had to have different sizes to fit different tins and glasses. There was a gap in the market for a more ergonomic strainer, and so along came the Hawthorne strainer, which beat the pack to become the ubiquitous cocktail strainer thanks to the coil, which fits into any shaker and can be really easily cleaned. It also has little hooks that balance it on top of the strainer. It takes its name from the Hawthorne Gentlemen's Cafe and Restaurant, a bar in Boston. The Julep has had a revival alongside many classic cocktails from that golden age of bartending, and is now often seen used with mixing glasses, whereas Hawthorne strainers are used with shaking tins. And finally we have the fine strainer, which really does what it says on the tin – it collects all of the smaller shards of ice left behind by the other strainer. It's usually not necessary for stirred drinks, as you should be moving the ice gently enough so it doesn't break into pieces small enough to pass through your Julep or Hawthorne, but is used for most shaken drinks (although personal preference can mean you like a few ice chips in your Daiquiri, for instance!).

4. JUICER

Those lemons and limes aren't going to juice themselves and, if you're making any quantity of cocktails at all, you'll soon get sick of squeezing them. A hand juicer is plenty for a home bar; in a higher volume bar environment an electric one is definitely worth spending money on because of the labour saved.

5. BARSPOON

This multitasker is both a mixing and a measuring utensil, so pretty darn useful. Again, you can get as fancy as you like with this, but basic ones are really cheap and easily found in hospitality shops. There's a bit of a knack to twirling it around the inside of the glass rather than churning it through the ice, and mastering it will help control the dilution and keep a silky smooth texture for your stirred-down drinks (plus you look like a boss) so definitely worth practising. The spoon part usually measures 5 ml (⅙ oz) so is really useful for those more finicky cocktail specs (which, by the way, is what bartenders often call cocktail recipes – short for 'specifications').

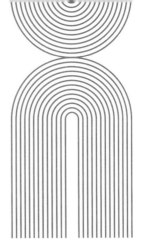

6. KNIFE AND/OR VEGETABLE PEELER (AND CHOPPING BOARD OF COURSE!)

It's always useful to have a knife (I prefer one with a serrated edge for cutting peel for 'twists' – see page 75) and a chopping board around when making drinks. A knife is necessary for cutting fruit wedges, trimming herbs and so on but some people prefer to use a vegetable peeler for twists. Whatever you use, just make sure it is sharp as you are way more likely to hurt yourself with a blunt tool since you have less control. Follow the same rules as for cooking – fingertips out of the way!

TEA TOWEL

Do not underestimate the importance of having a tea towel (dish towel) or cloth to hand (literally!). Alcohol, citrus and other juices are sticky and messy. A clean workspace is the mark of a good bartender, and your hands will thank you for keeping them dry.

BAR EQUIPMENT INESSENTIALS

(BUT THEY'RE NICE TO HAVE)

MIXING GLASS

Obviously you can get as fancy as you like with your mixing glass, and there are some beautiful ones out there, but it's also the least necessary piece of common bar equipment (especially for a home bar) as you just need a container to stir your booze on ice. One half of your shaker tin will absolutely work. Or honestly, I kind of believe homemade Martinis taste better when mixed in the glass section of a coffee plunger!

MUDDLER

Muddling is a messy and time-consuming endeavour, and I often find the resultant flavours rather overdone – I actually don't condone muddling the mint in a Mojito, for example, preferring to mix it through and let it infuse as it's sipped. A strong shake or churn on ice (stirring through on crushed ice, using the spoon to pull from the bottom up) gets the job done in my opinion, but many others swear by their muddlers and they can be useful to have around as general bashing tools.

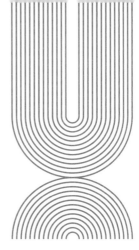

BLENDER

Every frozen drink can be made as an unfrozen drink (that is, just shaken), but there is something particularly satisfying about a frozen version on a hot day. Plus, you can make quite a few in one blender (usually around five or so) so they are good for parties. That said, there is another way to achieve frozen refreshment without a blender – see page 177.

MICROPLANE

These fine graters are great (pun intended) for garnishes. A cloud of shaved nutmeg or chocolate can finish off a dessert cocktail very nicely and is otherwise quite hard to achieve, but you'll also live without it.

TONGS/ICE SCOOP

I'm not telling you what to do when making drinks for yourself – if you want to lick each ice cube before putting it in your glass, far be it from me to stop you. However when serving drinks to guests, it's a good idea to have a hygienic way of handling your ice!

REUSABLE STRAWS/SKEWERS

Straws are generally only necessary where a glass is particularly long and thin, or a flamboyant garnish is in the way. Similarly, most garnishes can be propped against the edge of the glass but some need the help of a skewer to sit where they are supposed to. For these situations, consider investing in some reusable options, such as metal or glass – it will be less expensive in the long run and the sealife will thank you.

I am going to preface this by saying that the only true glassware essential (at least for a home bar) is whatever glassware you like drinking from. There's no point having 90 different styles of glasses if you'll only ever drink out of one or two. Alternatively you could have my problem – I love vintage glassware and have quite a collection, but they're not often standard sizes or shapes, so I'll drink a regular Highball out of a fluted goblet because it makes me happy to use that beautiful glass rather than a boring one!

In a bar it is important to have a range of glassware. It adds visual interest to rounds of drinks, and spreading your drink serves across different glasses means you shouldn't run out of any particular one on a busy night.

The following three are what I like to call 'the core range' – every drink can be served in one of them.

GLASSWARE ESSENTIALS

ROCKS GLASS

Otherwise known as a tumbler or an Old Fashioned glass, it is short and fairly wide. It can hold a spirit mixer or cocktail served on the rocks. These glasses come in all sorts of sizes; go for larger ones so you can fit in a big block of ice or just lots of cubed ice – around 350 ml (13 oz). These are sometimes called double rocks glasses. Single ones are good if you like drinking spirits on the rocks, or if you prefer to drink cocktails that are served 'up' (i.e. with no ice) in a rocks glass rather than in the usual stemware (general clumsiness will be accepted as an excuse for this, but not threatened masculinity).

HIGHBALL GLASS

Otherwise known as a tall glass – or Collins glass (which is technically slightly larger but often used interchangeably) – these glasses are tall and narrow and perfect for refreshing drinks, especially those with bubbles, such as soda water (club soda) or tonic. They are around the same volume as a large rocks glass but most cocktails served in rocks glasses are stirred or shaken then transferred to the glass, while a fair few tall drinks are 'built' in the glass then topped up, so you don't want to use one that is too large – an extra 30 ml (1 oz) of soda water could change the drink entirely if you don't also increase the volume of the other ingredients.

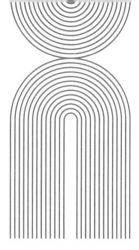

COCKTAIL/COUPE/MARTINI GLASS

What are cocktails about if not glamour, and to me these are the most opulent glasses. The legend goes that coupes were moulded in the shape of Marie Antoinette's left breast, but it actually turns out that they were invented, rather less sexily, about a century before she reigned, by an English monk. Originally used for Champagne, they were repurposed for cocktails and, although they lost their throne to the Martini glass through the mid and late 20th century, they have experienced a revival along with drinks from that pre- and immediately post-Prohibition era.

'Coupe' has become a catch-all term for curved and stemmed cocktail glasses.

The Martini glass has its own origin myth – that it was invented during Prohibition to make it easier to chuck your drink out quickly if the bar got raided – which is also not true. The Martini glass was really just a modern interpretation of the coupe, when straight lines were prized over curves in all things art and design.

It really does come down to aesthetics here; there are arguments for and against both shapes, but as long as it's big enough to fit your drink in (around 180 ml/6 oz for most standard recipes) and you like the look of it, who cares?

Setting Up Your Space

No bar setup will ever be perfect; there will always be space constraints, but we work with what we have. Here are a few things to consider for maximum speed and efficiency.

1. *What bottles will you use the most? Make sure these are easily reachable, and consider grouping ingredients used in popular or favourite cocktails together so they can be grabbed in quick succession.*

2. *Where are you keeping your glassware? If it's impractical to keep it in the fridge or freezer, fill it with ice to chill as you prepare the drink.*

3. *Is your ice source nearby? If not, consider investing in some form of insulated ice bucket so you don't have to run back and forth.*

4. *Have a bin nearby so you can keep your workspace clean and tidy – and ideally also a sink.*

5. *Most importantly, have a place for everything and return it there straight away after use. This is especially crucial when working in a bar with other people – there's nothing worse than thinking a bottle is 86'd and it turns out another bartender just left it somewhere else!*

A good bartender should be comfortable in their space – ruler of their domain. A bit of forethought about the nuts and bolts of your bar service will set you up for success and make it much easier to keep your guests satisfied, even when the orders start flowing in a little too quickly.

GLASSWARE INESSENTIALS

(BUT THEY'RE NICE TO HAVE)

WINE GLASS

You will most likely have these already, and I'll leave discussions of the various shapes and sizes to the wine experts, but I do know they make a dang good Spritz holder! The stem keeps your hands away from the drink, stopping the ice melting as quickly. You can actually use these quite interchangeably with Highball glasses – a G&T goes great in a wine glass as well, just ask the Spanish!

How to Hold Your Glass Like a Pro

Stemware is not only pretty, it's practical. It keeps your hot little hands away from your nice cold drink, keeping it cooler for longer! It also stops the glass from becoming grubby, and so just generally looks more elegant. It also keeps other odours out of the way when you're smelling your drink – whether you're tasting and assessing a spirit or wine, or just enjoying the spritz of citrus over your cocktail, your fingers can have lingering aromas on them, which can interfere.

CHAMPAGNE FLUTE

Flute glasses work well for Champagne cocktails, but they can also be served in a coupe. Conversely, if you don't have any coupes but you do have flutes, then chuck your Daiquiri in and happy days!

TASTING GLASSES

While not strictly cocktail glassware, these are useful for tasting and evaluating spirits, which is definitely part of the creative process. Furthermore, they're good for drinking shots out of (also sometimes part of the creative process).

NOVELTY GLASSES

Certain cocktails have bespoke glassware – if you are a massive fan of Mint Juleps, for example, it might behove you to invest in a Julep mug. Then there is the cacophony of tropical glassware out there – it might be frivolous, but anything that makes you feel like you're on holiday is all right by me. Just bear in mind a lot of these are larger than your standard rocks or Highball glass, so you may need to tweak drinks to fit – in a professional setting, always try your recipe in the glass you plan on serving it in before putting it on the menu, to make sure it looks presentable.

CHAPTER FOUR

HOW TO LEVEL UP
YOUR COCKTAILS

ZHUZH
MY DRINK

If a drink only contains booze and sugar it can be stirred, as the texture will be smooth and silky, which is ideal for showcasing a spirit-forward drink. But, if it contains anything else, such as juice, dairy or coffee, it should be shaken.

Once your bar is set for success, it's time to start making drinks! Mastering basic techniques and having attention to detail will be what lifts your libations above the pack. Organisation is also extremely important; whether you're hosting an intimate gathering or staffing a banquet hall, thinking through every step of the drinks you're serving, and figuring out ways you can make your life easier ahead of time, will save you from being caught with your pants down (a lesson I learned when turning up for a Valentine's Day event without oranges to garnish our Flame of Love cocktail – a pretty integral part given the name refers to flaming the orange zest!). So, here are my hints and tips for turning out the best possible version of your drinks while leaving yourself time to be the gracious host.

BASIC BARTENDING TECHNIQUES

SHAKING VERSUS STIRRING

To shake or to stir? That is the question. We all know it's a thorny debate when it comes to Martinis, but what does shaking or stirring actually do to your drink? The first serious bar I worked in actually had their cocktail list divided into shaken and stirred drinks, which seemed like an arbitrary distinction to a newbie like me – surely you want to give the guest an idea of what the drink will be like? The answer I got was that the technique used actually does relate to how you can expect the cocktail to be. The aim of both shaking and stirring is to chill and dilute the drink, but there are some key differences that impact the finished result.

Shaking chills and dilutes but also 'aerates' and 'emulsifies' – it creates air bubbles in the drink, and ensures all the ingredients are properly combined. Look at a Sour with egg white – I don't think you'd be very happy getting a stirred one with big glops of whites in there! And this is

where the bartender rule of thumb comes in. If a drink only contains booze and sugar it can be stirred, as the texture will be smooth and silky, which is ideal for showcasing a spirit-forward drink. But, if it contains anything else, such as juice, dairy or coffee, it should be shaken to take advantage of the aeration and produce a light and airy drink. You can see this most clearly when using something like pineapple juice or coffee, which actually produce a fluffy head on the drink, but even a well-shaken drink with citrus should have a little halo of bubbles promising extreme refreshment.

There's also a difference in temperature. Dave Arnold, whose book *Liquid Intelligence* is a must for any science-minded bartender, calculated that shaking is so violent that after around 15 seconds the drink reaches an equilibrium of chilling and diluting, i.e. it won't do much more of either even if you continue to shake. Stirring on the other hand is quite inefficient and would take closer to two minutes to reach the same point of equilibrium, which is much longer than people usually stir for. So, a stirred drink will be less cold and less diluted than a shaken drink. This might not sound particularly desirable, but I'm not saying the drink will be warm! It will still be chilled, but being slightly less so means that the nuances of the ingredients will be more perceptible.

Stirring also gives you much more control. You can choose, if you're serving something on ice for instance, to stir it a little less so it's not as diluted when being served and can evolve in the glass. The flipside to this element of control is that stirred drinks do take more care and attention – Arnold also proved that the quality and size of ice used doesn't really make a difference in shaking, whereas it does with stirred drinks, so use decent ice and plenty of it!

HOW TO SHAKE A DRINK

While many bartenders make quite a song and dance out of it, shaking a drink is easier than it looks. You can build your drink in either the smaller or the larger part of the shaker tin, but doing it in the larger part means splashing is less likely, as you then want to fill the smaller part of your shaker tin with ice – it's about the perfect amount to shake with. In one smooth move, bring the ice-filled part of the tin to rest inside the larger half. Ensure that both parts are lined up straight on one side. You can give them a bang at this point but, as long as they are lined up correctly and you keep a firm grip on them as you start to shake, they won't fly apart – the ice causes the metal to contract and forms a seal. As a precaution though, never shake directly towards someone's head! Shake with the smaller tin end towards you. I see a lot of people shaking up at one ear, but this puts a lot of strain on your shoulder. If you're planning on a bartending career, try to centre your shake in front of your chest to keep your physio happy. Shake as hard as you can (there's nothing worse

than a limp shake!) for around 10 seconds, or until your tin is frosted over. Again, to break the seal you can make a big performance of slapping the lip of the larger part of the tin but I find a gentle wiggle just as effective – hold the tin against your chest and push the small part diagonally to break the seal. And then you can move on to shaking two tins at once!

Double-shaking

If you are using egg whites in a cocktail, it gets controversial. Much like making a meringue, the light foam synonymous with this style of drink comes from breaking down the proteins in the egg, which means a fair amount of elbow grease! What you don't want, though, is to shake your cocktail so hard and for so long that it becomes over diluted. So some bright spark came up with the 'dry-shake' – shake all your ingredients without ice first to emulsify the egg, then add the ice and shake to chill and dilute. This is the most common technique I've encountered working in bars, but there is another (and probably most scientifically accurate) school of thought that advocates the 'reverse dry-shake'. The argument is that adding ice into the mixture, once you have emulsified the egg white, breaks down the foam you've built up, so you should actually shake everything except the whites on ice first, strain, then add the whites and dry-shake. Honestly, it's a bit of a mess around in the middle of a hectic service, and I've never had any problem getting a decent foamy head by just shaking really hard, but feel free to experiment!

BUILDING

Sometimes it's okay to take the easy way, and built drinks are a bartender's best friend when it comes to high volume. They are usually drinks that are already lengthened out, with soda water (club soda) or another non-alcoholic, bubbly ingredient, and served over ice.

Therefore the chilling, dilution and texture are taken care of with minimal effort on your part! A simple Highball is the most obvious example (a G&T or Whisk(e)y Soda, for instance), but there are also more complicated ones like Moscow Mules, Dark 'n' Stormys or Spritzes. For this style of drink, I like to add all the ingredients, including the mixer, before adding ice – it keeps them more consistent and pouring over ice can cause it to shift in the glass, meaning you add a different amount of mixer every time. Plus, it ensures all the ingredients are properly mixed – while the layered effect can look cool, you don't want to leave your guests with a mouthful of straight Aperol at the bottom of their Spritz! This way you can have them all measured out and lined up, and when your guests arrive all that's needed is a scoop of ice, a quick stir and a garnish – they're ideal for welcome drinks.

MUDDLING

I'm just going to say it – in a busy bar, muddling is a pain in the balls – or more accurately, the wrist and elbow. It takes longer, it's messy, it's inconsistent and it does nothing for my bartender RSI. Professionally, I would always suggest making a batch of fruit purée or a syrup, shrub or oleo to include fresh fruit in your drinks, and incorporating fresh herbs as a garnish. At home though, where a lot of those considerations don't matter too much, muddling is great! You can jazz up any drink you like with a few fresh berries or a ripe peach. Just make sure you do it in a metal tin or a VERY sturdy glass, and don't overdo it – you just want to gently press the ingredients to release their flavour, not pummel them into submission! Overzealous muddling can actually cause some unpleasantly bitter flavours to emerge, especially from citrus and herbs.

THROWING/ROLLING

While there are some proponents of 'throwing' drinks that are usually stirred, this technique is usually the preserve of the Bloody Mary. You assemble your drink in one half of the tin as usual, then add ice. A strainer (usually a Julep so it can fit in the tin at an angle rather than being wedged across) is placed inside the tin to hold the ice back. The liquid is then poured into another empty tin, then back over the ice, then into the empty tin again (repeat until dilution is achieved, usually around five times). The idea is to do this from a height, so that you are aerating the drink as well as chilling and diluting it, but in a much more gentle way than shaking. The main appeal of this is the theatrics – if you master it, you look like a boss. One tip is to start your pouring with both halves of the tin quite close together, and gradually move them apart – this way it's much easier to keep a steady stream pouring in the right spot instead of on your foot! If you don't quite trust yourself with this, your other option is just to 'roll' – seal the two halves of the tin as you would for shaking but just gently turn the tin over a few times so you're not causing any frothing of the liquid inside.

STRAINING

A few cocktails will be 'shake and dump' i.e. served on the ice they were shaken on (cool tip: this is the easiest way to get close to the effect of crushed ice if you can't be bothered actually crushing ice!), but most will either be served on fresh ice or served 'up' (with no ice). You generally always want to 'double-strain' drinks that are served up – i.e. use a Hawthorne strainer to hold the ice back in the tin but also pour through a fine strainer. This removes all the little ice shards, and is especially important for any drinks that have a fluffy head as those shards melt and ruin it. For drinks served on the rocks it's not as much of an issue.

ICE ICE BABY

There is one ingredient that is common to almost every drink that gets passed over the bar, and usually makes up about a quarter of it, and yet often gets overlooked – ice. Ice and cocktails go hand in hand. In fact, during the Gold Rush in Australia, ice was imported all the way from Canada just so people could show off how wealthy they were by how frosty their Sherry Cobbler was! The first ice machine was invented in the mid-1800s and we haven't looked back to room-temperature drinks since.

So. The big question. Are bartenders trying to rip you off by putting lots of ice in your drink? The short answer is absolutely not. The simplified long answer is that ice keeps ice cold, and therefore keeps the liquid cold, so the more ice there is, the colder and less diluted your drink will be. Asking for less ice just means that you will get more mixer in your glass, and the whole thing will end up a watery mess much faster! It has absolutely zero effect on how much booze there is in there. This is also why drinks that have been prediluted, i.e. cocktails that have been stirred or shaken already, should be served on the biggest block of ice you can get your hands on, as you just want the drink to remain cold and not dilute much more. This is one situation where size does matter.

As an industry, we are in a glorious Second Ice Age. Bartenders really care about the ice going into drinks – you might have seen or used beautifully big clear blocks of ice. They usually come from specialised equipment that freezes massive blocks of ice from one end to another, meaning all of the impurities get forced out of the block rather than getting trapped in the middle and going cloudy. A way to achieve this on a budget is to freeze water in a cooler/chilly bin with the top off, as it will freeze from the open end first, and you can chop off the end that goes cloudy. To be perfectly honest though, in a home bar situation I'd say to just invest in some 2.5 cm (1 inch) ice moulds for shaking and stirring, and big blocks or ball ice moulds that fit your glassware for serving, and freeze way more than you think you need! And if you're in a pinch and can only get your hands on party ice, don't panic – just take that into consideration and shake or stir for less time.

VISUALLY APPEALING DRINKS

You drink with your eyes first, so it's worth putting some thought into the presentation of your drinks. And, at the end of the day, cocktails are fun – so they should look it, too!

GARNISHES

Garnishes can enhance a drink aesthetically, aromatically and/or flavour wise, but they need to add something. If your garnish is looking sad, just leave it off. Obviously some drinks have very specific garnishes, which will be explored in their recipes, but here are some common ones to master.

Wedges

Simple but often badly executed, I favour wedges over slices for standard spirit mixers as people can choose to squeeze them into their drink. They should therefore be thick enough to squeeze! Cut the bottom off your fruit, then halve it from pole to pole. Cut in half again, then cut into each quarter at a 45-degree angle to form the wedge. These should then be trimmed, especially for any fruits with

seeds – cut along the long edge of your wedge to remove pith and any seeds, and generally just make it neater. Basically any citrus can be prepared this way (lemons and limes of course, but also oranges and grapefruits) but they should be used on the day they are cut.

Twists

These are probably the most common cocktail garnish, as the aroma of the citrus oils really brings drinks to life. You can use either a knife or a vegetable peeler, and it works for basically all citrus (although bear in mind lime rind is quite bitter so is usually avoided). Cut from one pole of the fruit to the other on a slight angle, moving the knife or peeler away from you. On smaller pieces of fruit you might have to wrap almost the whole way around to get a decent length, but you should be able to get six or so twists out of a reasonable-sized orange. If you use a knife, it usually cuts a little deeper and takes lots of white pith off as well, in which case hold the twist, skin side down, on your chopping board and shave more of the pith off, again moving the knife away from you (and fingers behind it!).

Vegetable peelers tend to give the right thickness at first go. You can then choose to keep the twist 'rustic' – i.e. untrimmed, which I usually do when serving on the rocks – or trim it down. You can get creative at this point, or just keep it simple and cut off the rough edges, slimming it down. This tends to look better in more delicate stemmed glasses.

Before garnishing with your twist, you want to expel its oils over the drink. Hold it about 5–7.5 cm (2–3 inches) above your glass with the skin side pointed at the glass, and sharply fold it. If it is a nice, fresh, firm piece of fruit then you should see (and smell!) a lovely spray anointing your cocktail. Give it a twist and add it to the drink, anchoring it to the rim of the glass if possible so it doesn't get up the drinker's nose! (See page 91 for a flaming twist.)

Wheels and Ribbons

Suspending fruit through the drinks can create a really beautiful look, especially in larger glassware – it's an easy way to level up a fairly simple drink like a G&T. For this I cut thin wheels of citrus and use two or three in the drink. Another favourite is a ribbon of cucumber – run a vegetable peeler down the length of the cucumber and wrap the ribbon around the inside of the glass.

Dehydrated wheels are also quite common these days and are a good way to save time and reduce wastage. Cut wheels as thin as you can manage and dry them – it's easiest to do this in a dehydrator of course, but you can also put them in an oven on the lowest heat, and just keep an eye on them. They take about a day, and can be done in batches. Some argue against them because the drying process means they don't have much aroma left, but they still look really pretty and so are great for an easy pop of colour, and much less hassle in the middle of a busy service than messing around with fresh fruit. They also float on drinks much more easily than fresh wheels! They

will last for months in an airtight container so consider it the next time you have some fruit going to waste. Citrus works of course but also pineapples (cut the wheel in half), plums, mandarins (cut segments almost in half so they open out into a butterfly shape), strawberries – you name it – you can probably dehydrate it!

Herbs

Herbs are absolutely my favourite garnish as they are cheap (free if you forage!) and easy, but add such fragrance and another layer of savoury flavour to drinks. Mint should be picked ahead of time, taking the larger leaves off the stem and keeping them aside for drinks that require them, such as Mojitos, and leaving the 'sprig' – the little bunch of smaller leaves at the top. The stem should then be trimmed down a little to make it easier to handle; most other herbs can be left whole but also trimmed to fit the glass. Before use, give them a gentle smack across the back of your hand to release the aroma, and arrange in the glass. Bunches should always be generous, and placed right beside the straw so the drinker is basically burying their nose in them as they take a sip. Delightful.

Cherries and Olives

Not in the same drink, of course, but I have the same thing to say about both – get good-quality ones! Nothing ruins your perfectly balanced Manhattan quicker than a glob of radioactively pink cherry juice at the end, and less-than-delicious olives are a sad accompaniment to a Martini. I like morello cherries, which are slightly sour, or the Luxardo brand is a safe bet for maraschinos. Stick to green olives in cocktails as black olives tend to overpower everything; I use local manzanilla olives in brine.

Bitters and Aromatics

A dash or some dots of bitters across the top of your drink can allow you to flex your artistic talent – this works particularly well on drinks with a foamy head as you can use a skewer to draw patterns. Otherwise, having some bitters or other aromatics, such as absinthe or vermouth, in a little atomiser bottle can allow you to spritz the top of your drink to give it some lovely top notes without needing any fresh fruit or herbs around – great if you're disorganised and tend to cocktail on the fly.

Rims

What is a Margarita without her crowning halo of moreish salt? But there are more to rims than just this; Tajin seasoning is a welcome addition to many mezcal drinks, or cinnamon sugar works well with whisk(e)y. Rimming is potentially a misleading name – it should be on the outside of the glass only, not on the rim itself and definitely not on the inside, as it will fall into the drink and change it entirely. A strong shake after dabbing should remove any rogue granules sitting on the wrong side. Use a wedge of fruit to wet the outside of the glass – I usually just do halfway, but quite a thick rim, so the drinker can choose whether to have some or not with each sip – and then dab the rim in your powdered substance of choice.

Other Garnishes

There is plenty of room to be creative with garnishes and often things that would otherwise go to waste can be repurposed. If you're making a pineapple syrup, for example, save the fronds and use them to garnish the glass for a tropical look. Mandarin and other citrus peels can be dehydrated and blitzed up, then added to sugar to make sherbet rims. Left-over pulp from syrups can also be dehydrated and turned into fruit leather, because who doesn't love a snack with their drink? And berries and soft herbs that might not make it to the next round of drinks can be frozen into ice cubes for a pop of colour.

WASHLINES

This simply refers to where the liquid sits beneath the rim of the glass. Too low and it looks stingy; too high and it makes the drink difficult to carry, resulting in spillage all down the side of the glass and a generally messy-looking drink. Drinks should always be tested in their serving glassware before they are served to guests to ensure they sit at a nice level, and that means that if it isn't sitting right then something has gone wrong. An ingredient might have been missed or overpoured, the drink might be overdiluted. Either way, a drink not sitting nicely in the glass is a warning sign. In the best case scenario you just need to add an extra cube or two of ice to fill it and make it look generous; in the worst case, the drink has to be remade.

COLOUR

One of the bars that I worked in had a rule against 'brown liquid in a glass'. While brown liquid in a glass can be exceedingly delicious, this bar was a bright and fun garden bar so it just didn't work (whereas in a dark basement bar with leather armchairs, brown drinks might be the perfect fit). Sometimes a drink can be really tasty but just doesn't come out a great colour, especially if you're using homemade ingredients, so you'll never get the 'ooh' factor as it comes over to the table. At this point you might want to add a purely decorative garnish (edible flowers are always a winner) or think about adding a coloured ingredient that will work with the flavour profile (a bar spoon of Aperol has often got me out of this exact predicament). As a last resort, just put it in a coloured glass or ceramic mug instead!

Cocktails take time. If you need a drink IMMEDIATELY then please just order a beer. But, there are a few things you can do to get ahead and ensure speed and efficiency of service.

GETTING AHEAD

PREP

Most bars have a setup bartender who will come in an hour or two before the bar is open to do 'prep' (lucky ones have dedicated prep days!) and the same can be done when hosting at home. Juicing citrus, picking herbs, cutting fruit for garnish and making homemade ingredients should all be done ahead of time. You obviously can't get too far ahead of yourself – citrus juice and wedges last around a day refrigerated, soft herbs around three, and garnish twists are better done to order as they dry out quite quickly. Adjust how much you prepare depending on whether you're expecting a busy night to try and limit wastage – better to prep slightly less and cut/juice a little towards the end of the night, than have to chuck out a lot of unused fruit.

BATCHING

This used to be a dirty word – it was seen as not real bartending if you weren't picking up every individual bottle to make every individual drink. Thankfully that stigma is fading, with bartenders embracing the speed and consistency it affords. You might be thinking of a Punch or jug-style group serve, and that's certainly a form of batching, but it works on a more individualised level as well. Stable cocktail ingredients (i.e., everything except fresh juices) can be batched together so that instead of pouring 40 ml of X, 20 ml of Y and 10 ml of Z plus 30 ml of lime juice for one drink, you can just pour 70 ml of XYZ from one bottle, add your lime juice and shake. The former is good for events where everyone is arriving at a similar time and you know exactly what is being served; the latter works in a general bar setting where you can batch popular drinks ahead of time but still serve them to order.

A Few Things to Consider when Batching

1. *It's easiest to think of your drinks recipe in parts as opposed to specific measurements when scaling up, e.g. 2 parts whisk(e)y, 1 part vermouth. This way you can make a batch of any size you like without overly complicated mathematics. Otherwise, if you know exactly how many drinks you need to make, you can just multiply each ingredient by that number.*

2. *Make sure you measure accurately – small mistakes become big ones when measured up!*

3. *Always shake or stir your batch before using – if it sits for a while, then heavier ingredients like liqueurs and syrups will sink, so make sure everything is fully incorporated before pouring.*

4. *Alcohol is a preservative, so batches with homemade ingredients will last for a while but not forever – usually a few weeks, but try to keep them in the fridge. Batches that are quite low ABV (alcohol by volume), for instance with a high proportion of vermouth, should also be kept in the fridge. Never batch with citrus unless you know you will use the whole batch that day – otherwise it can be added just before shaking.*

5. *Will you have time to shake or stir? Drinks with fresh juice will always need to be shaken, but stirred or all-booze drinks can be prediluted ahead of time. Just measure one out as normal, stir it until the desired dilution and then measure its new volume. The difference in volume is the amount of water that needs to be added per drink in the batch. Make sure prediluted batches are chilled before serving, preferably in the freezer to achieve an effect closer to that if they had been stirred.*

6. *Add any fizzy ingredients (soda water/club soda, sparkling wine etc.) at the last moment before serving.*

BUILDING A ROUND

Unfortunately, nine times out of ten your guests aren't all going to be drinking the same thing. So, how do you get a range of drinks up quickly and efficiently so no one gets grumpy that they had to wait longer than Janice from HR did for their drink?

Get Your Garnish Ready First

This is my number one mantra. You don't want to have a drink sitting ready and then start messing around with cutting fruit or twists. Get every garnish you'll need close to hand, ready to be popped on top.

Line up Your Glassware/Shaker Tin/Mixing Glasses

This is a good hack especially if your memory is as bad as mine – getting out all the glasses you'll need straight away should jog your memory as to which drinks and how many are on order. Note that I don't mean to grab cocktail glassware out of the fridge at this point – that should always be done at the last moment – but if there are any drinks being built directly into the glass.

Start with the Cheapest Ingredients

I'll hold my hands up here and say I don't always remember to do this but it's a good rule of thumb especially when starting out, as any mistakes will be less costly. So if, for instance, you're making a couple of drinks with lime juice, then measure that into each shaker tin at the same time, so you don't have to put the bottle down and pick it back up again.

Pour Your Liquor in Order

Another little trick to minimise the chance of mistakes is to always pour your spirits in the same order. I do mine from 'lightest' to 'heaviest', so I start with vodka, then gin, then white rum and so on up to whisk(e)y. Do it however makes sense to you – maybe you would think of dark rum as 'heavier' than whisk(e)y for example, but the main point is that if you get distracted and lose your train of thought then you won't forget what is in each glass or tin! Do this until your drinks are all 'built', i.e. all of the necessary ingredients have been poured into each one (make sure to rinse your jigger between strong-tasting or sticky pours).

Add Your Mixer

Ice or mixer first is the bartender equivalent of the chicken and the egg dilemma, but let me give you two arguments for doing mixer first. I've discussed this above when talking about building technique but, basically, I think of ice in drinks as a ticking time bomb – as soon as you add it, the drink starts inching closer to death. A bit dramatic maybe, but if you get distracted or have to do something else quickly – is that a glass smashing?! – then you can pause the round with no harm done. So add any soda water (club soda), tonic, sparkling wine or so on to the drinks that require it before ice.

Shake and Stir

Assuming you're using decent ice, you can add some to your mixing glass and let it sit for a minute while you shake your shaken drinks. The shaken drinks can then be strained off the ice into serving glassware. The stirred drinks can then be stirred and strained off the ice into serving glassware.

Add Ice

Add ice to any built drinks and any of the
shaken or stirred drinks that are being served
on the rocks. Do this gently to avoid splashing.

Garnish and Serve!

It seems like a lot to get your head around
but practice makes perfect and at some point
muscle memory does take over. On quiet nights
you can practise making rounds quickly, picking
up the bottles but not actually pouring them,
just to get used to the rhythm. Bartending
really is a little like dancing; once you master
the foundational steps you can jazz it up and
have some fun with your style of service!

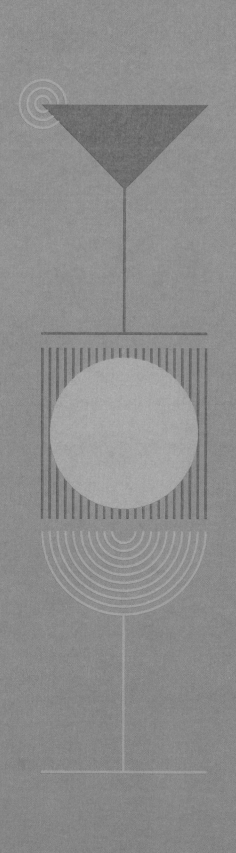

THE
RECIPES

ABOUT THE RECIPES

Drinks categories have a messy family dynamic. There's always the oddball cousin, the black sheep, the exception that proves the rule. Any attempts to parcel them neatly leave you tearing your hair out – believe me, I've tried! That said, I find it much more useful to group drinks by their makeup of strong, sweet and bitter or sour – their DNA, if you will – than by their base spirit.

A Daiquiri has much more in common with a Cosmopolitan than it does with a Piña Colada or an Eggnog. Nobody ever really just thinks 'I want a rum drink' with no further qualifications, but they might well think 'It's hot, I want something super refreshing!'. So, that's how I've divided up the recipes in this book – you can choose what mood you're in and take it from there! Of course some drinks will straddle multiple categories, but not everything in life fits neatly into a box and that's what makes it interesting.

Each section will contain the Famous Ones – trailblazers that have stood the test of time to become cocktail blueprints, essentially, and deserve a proper exploration of their history and influence. Then there are the Honourable Mentions (popular variations) and Fun Twists – lesser-known drinks that showcase how you can easily expand your repertoire with just a few substitutions. There's no way I can cover every cocktail I'd like to here, but it should be plenty to get you started, and I've arranged them in rough chronological order within each chapter to give an idea of how they all flow from one to another.

Each recipe has a diagram breaking down the strong, sweet and sour or bitter elements in the drink. In the interest of simplicity, where an ingredient brings more than one taste to the table (for example vermouth is always sweet and a little bitter) I have placed it on the side of the triangle with it's most dominant characteristic/the role it is playing in that particular recipe, but refer to the Venn Diagram on page 20 to help understand how some ingredients bring more than one element to the table.

A NOTE ON FOLLOWING THE RECIPES

I'm a cowboy of a cook. I'll flick through a few books to get some inspiration, but I rarely follow recipes from start to finish (and I'll sometimes take a few wrong turns along the way, but that's okay!). I'll blend techniques and flavour combinations from different recipes or cuisines – my partner often looks a bit worried at some of my crazier fusions – but it (almost!) always ends up being tasty. The more you understand the Taste Triangle (see page 18) and the fundamentals of flavour (see page 6), the easier it will be to experiment, so using these recipes as a base can help build your confidence to deviate from them. Tasting ingredients individually is the best way to understand how to use them to good effect. If you are altering an ingredient by substituting something in, always use a little less than is called for in the recipe to give yourself some breathing room to balance it.

A NOTE ON RATIOS

There is no one certain way to balance a cocktail. As Gaz Regan says of the Negroni, 'you can slap my wrist and call me Deborah if it doesn't also work no matter what ratios you use'. Not all cocktails are quite as lucky as the Negroni, but the same combination of ingredients can strike a good balance in multiple different ratios. Two of my go-to ratios are:

1. Four parts strong, one part sweet, two parts bitter or sour

2. Two parts strong, three-quarters part sweet, three-quarters part bitter or sour

These work in basically all sour-style cocktails and a lot of others – the first will give you a zippier, fresher drink and the second will give a rounder, richer one. Even drinks that don't follow these ratios in their 'correct' recipes taste pretty good using either of these formulas, so they're always a good place to start.

SHORT
AND BOOZY

These are the heavy hitters of the cocktail world, sometimes known as the original cocktails. Spirit-forward and stirred down, they are some of the most difficult to master; with no juices involved there is nowhere to hide. This does mean that they are the ideal vehicles to showcase a special bottle you might have. The balancing element in these drinks is generally bitterness rather than sourness, either through cocktail bitters or ingredients like vermouth, which have a bitter edge to them.

Low and No:

These drinks are difficult to make entirely non-alcoholic. Although there are some good non-alcoholic spirit replacements on the market now, they usually come into their own when mixed with other flavours. However, it is easy to reduce the alcohol content by 'reversing' these drinks – using more of the lower-alcohol ingredients, such as vermouth, and just a small amount of the spirit for backbone. I often prefer Reverse Manhattans!

THE OLD FASHIONED

The Old Fashioned is really the closest drink to the original definition of a cocktail (liquor, sugar, bitters and water), but it obviously had to go out of fashion for it to become old-fashioned! It originally went under the less judgemental name 'Whiskey Cocktail' and was referred to as such for several decades, served up (i.e. with no ice) and usually as an 'eye opener' in the morning.

So what happened for this simple but delicious drink to become passé? Well, by the 1870s bartenders had begun to have more access to liqueurs and other flavour modifiers. They got a bit excited and started pumping out 'Improved' Whiskey Cocktails. As with any attempt at modernisation there were those who resisted it. Plenty of people have laid claim to the Old Fashioned name, most notably the Pendennis Club in Louisville, where the story goes that a grumpy local bourbon distiller asked for a cocktail 'the old-fashioned way' – i.e. none of your fancy new-fangled bullsh*t – so the bartender took it back to basics (with the addition of ice – so clearly the grumpy bourbon distiller wasn't against all modern comforts) and the cocktail we know and love was born.

Pro Tip:
While more synonymous with whisk(e)y these days, you can base an Old Fashioned on any spirit you like! Play around with cocktail bitters that reflect the flavour profile of the spirit you're using – I love using nutty ones with rum.

You may have seen bartenders dash a sugar cube with bitters (add multiple dashes of bitters to a sugar cube to dissolve it) and muddle it in the bottom of the glass. You can absolutely do it this way; I just find that you have more control by using sugar syrup, and the resulting texture is smoother with no rogue undissolved sugar crystals.

>

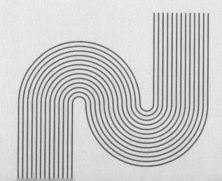

Ingredients Note:
[1] I always ask if the guest has a preference for an Old Fashioned – it would traditionally be American whiskey (bourbon or rye) but I've found a lot of guests expect Scottish whisky these days.

INGREDIENTS

60 ml (2 oz) whisk(e)y[1]

7.5 ml (¼ oz) sugar syrup (see page 45)

2 dashes Angostura bitters

2 dashes orange bitters

Ice: large block

Garnish: orange zest twist (see page 75)

EQUIPMENT

Glassware: rocks glass

Jigger

Mixing glass

Julep strainer

Bar spoon

METHOD

Place all the ingredients in a mixing glass and stir until desired dilution (I like to underdilute slightly and let it develop over ice in the glass). Fold your twist over the top to expel the oils, then use as a garnish.

Whiskey — Sugar Syrup

Bitters

OAXACA OLD FASHIONED

Invented by New York bartender Phil Ward in 2007, this shows how easily new life can be breathed into this ageless cocktail. Mezcal was just becoming popular outside of Mexico, so Ward introduced it in a known cocktail format and as an accent spirit to make it approachable.

Ingredients Notes:
[1] *I also like to add a couple of dashes of locally made agave and pink grapefruit bitters.*

[2] *Flaming is not necessary but it is the original serve. To achieve this, cut a coin-sized piece of zest. Bend it skin-forward towards the drink with one hand, and hold a lighter a few cm (couple of inches) under the zest with the other. Let the zest warm under the flame for a second and then quickly squeeze it so the oils expel through the flame for a moment of high drama!*

INGREDIENTS

45 ml (1½ oz) reposado tequila

15 ml (½ oz) mezcal

5 ml (⅙ oz) agave syrup

2 dashes Angostura bitters[1]

Ice: large block

Garnish: flamed[2] orange zest twist (see page 75)

EQUIPMENT

Glassware: rocks glass

Jigger

Mixing glass

Julep strainer

Bar spoon

METHOD

Place all the ingredients in a mixing glass and stir until desired dilution (I like to under-dilute slightly and let it develop over ice in the glass). Fold your twist over the top, flame and expel the oils, then use as a garnish.

Tequila
Mezcal
Agave

Angostura Bitters

91

◡

THE COFFEE HOUSE

The original recipe called for equal parts regular coffee and rye whiskey, with some sugar and bitters. It's assumed it would have been served warm but the book the recipe was from was fairly tongue-in-cheek and concentrated more on gently mocking the temperance movement than giving clear instructions on how to make the drinks! However, modern bartenders, such as Michael Madrusan, decided to take another look at it and reimagined it more as a coffee-flavoured Old Fashioned.

Ingredients Note:
[1] I also like to add a couple of dashes of locally made nutty bitters.

INGREDIENTS

40 ml (1¼ oz) rye whiskey

15 ml (½ oz) coffee liqueur

2 dashes orange bitters[1]

Ice: large block

Garnish: orange zest twist (see page 75)

EQUIPMENT

Glassware: rocks glass

Jigger

Mixing glass

Julep strainer

Bar spoon

METHOD

Place all the ingredients in a mixing glass and stir until desired dilution (I like to under-dilute slightly and let it develop over ice in the glass). Fold your twist over the top to expel the oils, then use as a garnish.

Whiskey / Coffee Liqueur / Bitters

THE SAZERAC

The Sazerac story ended up being a little more complicated than I had first realised. The one I had always heard was made famous by Stanley Clisby Arthur, who wrote a book on famous New Orleans cocktails. He said that Antoine Peychaud, a pharmacist, liked to serve and drink his eponymous bitters mixed with Cognac in little cups (called 'coquetiers'). Meanwhile, another New Orleans–based businessman was importing brandy, specifically Sazerac de Forge & Fils Cognac. It all gets a bit fuzzy here but, basically, that same man is also involved with the Merchant's Exchange Coffee House which, despite the name, is a bar. There, at some point around the 1850s, they started mixing the Cognac with Peychaud's bitters, and this would have been known as a 'Sazerac cocktail'. Around the 1870s, absinthe was the cool new cocktail ingredient on the block and that got added to the mix. The story then goes that phylloxera, a root disease that crippled France's wine and brandy industry, made Cognac hard to come by and so rye was substituted, eventually becoming the norm.

Peychaud's coquetiers have also been promoted by New Orleans as the root of the word cocktail, conveniently crowning the city the birthplace of the cocktail. David Wondrich, that great debunker of myths, is widely acknowledged as the foremost cocktail historian in the world, and as such he has a rather annoying habit of actually checking dates and looking at facts. He pointed out that seeing as the first written instance of the word 'cocktail' was in 1806 and Peychaud was born in 1803, he probably can't claim it. He also pointed out that the whole Peychaud's–coffee house–Cognac–Sazerac cocktail link is pure conjecture. The first written reference to a Sazerac cocktail is in 1899, and it is definitely a rye cocktail.

>

93

Pro Tip:
You can use an atomiser, or just 'rinse' the glass with absinthe by rolling a small amount around the glass (see page 117), but filling your serving glass with ice and adding the absinthe will not only chill the glass but also release some more subtle flavours from a good-quality absinthe – this is also why water is usually added to absinthe when it is being drunk by itself.

INGREDIENTS

10–15 ml (⅓–½ oz) absinthe, to rinse

60 ml (2 oz) rye whiskey

10 ml (⅓ oz) sugar syrup (see page 44)

4 dashes Peychaud's bitters

Served up (no ice)

Garnish: lemon zest twist (see page 75)

EQUIPMENT

Glassware: small rocks glass (a shot or tasting glass is optional to serve the absinthe on the side)

Jigger

Mixing glass or another rocks glass

Bar spoon

Julep strainer

METHOD

Fill a serving glass with ice and add the absinthe, drizzling around as much as possible. Give it a stir and leave to chill. Place all the other ingredients in your mixing glass or other rocks glass (traditionally it is prepared in two rocks glasses but a mixing glass works just fine!). Fill with ice and stir. Once chilled and diluted, strain the absinthe into the shot glass and discard the ice; strain the drink into the serving glass. Cut a coin-sized piece of lemon zest. Fold the zest sharply over the drink from a height to expel the oils, then discard. Serve your Sazerac with the absinthe on the side (if you like!).

THE NEW YORK SAZERAC (OR SPLIT BASE SAZERAC)

Dale DeGroff, a bartender and author at the forefront of the craft cocktail revolution we're experiencing now, included a split base Sazerac as a nod to the Cognac origins tale in his 2002 book *Craft of the Cocktail* (which was my bible when I was starting out in the industry). The Sazerac never disappeared in the US, as much as it may have fallen out of fashion, but for many international bartenders, this may have been the first time they'd ever heard of the drink, and not realised this recipe was unusual. DeGroff is from New York, and so the differentiation between his version and the rye-based New Orleans one slipped into bartender parlance in the UK and Australia (or at least this is my supposition!).

Split Base

A cocktail that uses two or more spirits as the 'strong' part of the cocktail.

INGREDIENTS

10–15 ml (⅓–½ oz) absinthe, to rinse

30 ml (1 oz) rye whiskey

30 ml (1 oz) Cognac

7.5 ml (¼ oz) sugar syrup (see page 44)

4 dashes Peychaud's bitters

Served up (no ice)

Garnish: lemon zest to twist and discard (see page 75)

EQUIPMENT

Glassware: small rocks glass (a shot or tasting glass is optional to serve the absinthe on the side)

Jigger

Mixing glass or another rocks glass

Bar spoon

Julep strainer

METHOD

Fill a serving glass with ice and add the absinthe, drizzling around as much as possible. Give it a stir and leave to chill. Add all the other ingredients to your mixing glass or other rocks glass (traditionally it is prepared in two rocks glasses but a mixing glass works just fine!). Fill with ice and stir. Once chilled and diluted, strain the absinthe into the shot glass and discard the ice; strain the drink into the serving glass. Cut a coin-sized piece of lemon zest. Fold the zest sharply over the drink from a height to expel the oils, then discard. Serve your Sazerac with the absinthe on the side (if you like!).

‿

LA LOUISIANE

Sometimes called a De La Louisiane or a Cocktail à la Louisiane, it takes its name from the restaurant La Louisiane, where it was the house cocktail. It was included in the same cocktail book as the Sazerac, *Stanley Clisby Arthur's Famous New Orleans Drinks and How to Mix 'Em*, which came out in 1937, but this cocktail has never enjoyed the same reach as its more famous peer. The sweet component of the drink is made up of vermouth and liqueur rather than just sugar syrup, making it richer.

Ingredients Note:
[1] Benedictine is one of France's many herbal liqueurs made by monks. It is more honey-sweet than drinks like Chartreuse, and has a warm liquorice flavour that works well with the absinthe and spicy rye.

INGREDIENTS

50 ml (1⅔ oz) rye whiskey

25 ml (⅘ oz) sweet vermouth

10 ml (⅓ oz) Benedictine[1]

3 dashes Peychaud's bitters

3 dashes absinthe

Served up (no ice)

Garnish: 1–3 cherries

EQUIPMENT

Glassware: coupe or Martini glass

Mixing glass

Jigger

Bar spoon

Julep strainer

METHOD

Add all the ingredients to a mixing glass and stir until chilled and diluted. Use the Julep strainer to hold the ice back in the mixing glass and pour into your chilled coupe glass. Garnish with one cherry in the bottom of the glass or three on a skewer, depending how much you like cherries!

Whiskey / Vermouth Benedictine Absinthe / Bitters

THE MANHATTAN

The Manhattan actually enjoyed quite a clear-cut and entertaining origin story until fairly recently. The story went that Jennie Jerome (who would go on to become Lady Randolph Churchill) hosted a party at the Manhattan Club in 1874 to celebrate the nomination of a New York governor and called for whiskey and vermouth to celebrate. The only problem is, as cocktail historian David Wondrich pointed out, Jennie Jerome was in England and pretty busy with the birth of her child Winston Churchill when this party took place. What is true is that the Manhattan Club, a private members' club, was once situated in a building that had previously been owned by Jennie's father, and so when Winston Churchill became a well-known figure, this small link grew legs into a good story. It is possible that the drink was invented at the Manhattan Club specifically, but there is no real way to verify that, and there are several other plausible claims. What does make sense is that there were massive waves of Italian immigration to the US around this time, and so Italians would have brought their beloved sweet vermouth with them. It was only a matter of time before some bright spark mixed it with the local whiskey and some bitters as a twist on the foundational American cocktail – the Old Fashioned.

Pro Tip:
The vermouth portion of the cocktail is what differentiates a 'dry', 'perfect' and 'sweet' Manhattan. Unlike in the Martini, a dry Manhattan is literally one made with dry vermouth, a perfect Manhattan is made with both sweet and dry, and a sweet Manhattan is made with sweet vermouth. If you just ask for a Manhattan, the standard is sweet. Please don't be afraid of this, it does not mean overly sugary – sweet vermouth still has a nice bitterness to it, and it rounds out the spicy rye. A perfect Manhattan is a good option if you are using bourbon rather than rye, as the dry vermouth balances out the slightly sweeter whiskey base.

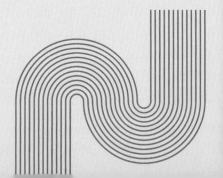

INGREDIENTS

Ingredients Note:
[1] *Many of the original references to the Manhattan don't specify bourbon or rye, saying only 'whiskey'. New York was, at that time, a rye-drinking city so I stick with that unless specified otherwise.*

50 ml (1⅔ oz) rye whiskey[1]

20 ml (⅔ oz) sweet vermouth

2 dashes Angostura bitters

Served up (no ice)

Garnish: orange or lemon zest twist (see page 75) and a cherry

EQUIPMENT

Glassware: coupe or Martini glass

Mixing glass

Jigger

Bar spoon

Julep strainer

METHOD

Add all the ingredients to a mixing glass and stir until chilled and diluted. Use the Julep strainer to hold the ice back in the mixing glass and pour into your chilled coupe glass. Folding a twist over the top to expel the oils over the top of the drink will really brighten it up (discard the zest), but the traditional garnish is a cherry, as a nod to the maraschino liqueur featured in some early recipes.

Whiskey

Vermouth

Bitters

BOBBY BURNS

A Rob Roy, named after a famous Scottish outlaw, is simply a Manhattan made with scotch, and the Bobby Burns takes it one step further by adding a herbal liqueur alongside the vermouth. It is often drunk on Burns Night to celebrate the famous Scottish bard, but it has been suggested that the drink was actually named after a cigar salesman in New York – somewhat less romantic.

INGREDIENTS

Ingredients Note:
[1] A less smoky blended whisky works well but feel free to experiment with your favourite bottle.

40 ml (1⅓ oz) Scottish whisky[1]

20 ml (¾ oz) sweet vermouth

10 ml (⅓ oz) Benedictine or Drambuie

2 dashes orange bitters

Served up (no ice)

Garnish: lemon zest twist (see page 75) and a cherry

EQUIPMENT

Glassware: coupe or Martini glass

Mixing glass

Jigger

Bar spoon

Julep strainer

METHOD

Add all the ingredients to a mixing glass and stir until chilled and diluted. Use the Julep strainer to hold the ice back in the mixing glass and pour into your chilled coupe glass. Fold your twist over the top to expel the oils, then discard and add a cherry to garnish.

Scotch — *Drambuie/Benedictine* — *Vermouth*

Bitters

⌣

EL PRESIDENTE

The Cuban answer to a Manhattan, this cocktail shows that rum drinks can be just as sophisticated as the rest of them! It has been around since the early 1900s, and was apparently named after the Cuban president at the time.

INGREDIENTS

40 ml (1⅓ oz) white rum[1]

20 ml (⅔ oz) white vermouth[2]

10ml (⅓ oz) dry curaçao[3]

Bar spoon grenadine (see page 47)

Served up (no ice)

Garnish: orange zest twist (see page 75)

EQUIPMENT

Glassware: coupe or Martini glass

Mixing glass

Jigger

Bar spoon

Julep strainer

Ingredients Notes:
[1] *Choose something fruity and flavourful.*

[2] *The original recipe called for a vermouth from Chambéry – Dolin works well. Make sure you use a white vermouth – dry vermouth doesn't work.*

[3] *This is quite a delicately balanced drink so your orange liqueur does have to be quite a dry one, otherwise add less.*

METHOD

Add all the ingredients to a mixing glass and stir until chilled and diluted. Use the Julep strainer to hold the ice back in the mixing glass and pour into your chilled coupe glass. Fold your twist over the top to expel the oils, then use as a garnish.

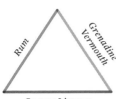

Rum

Grenadine Vermouth

Orange Liqueur

THE MARTINI

While it may seem odd to anyone who has tried the modern versions of both drinks, the Martini evolved from the Manhattan, which was the first cocktail to combine spirits and vermouth. The Martini's direct ancestor is the Martinez, which is listed in Jerry Thomas's *Bartenders Guide* in 1887 as combining bitters, maraschino, vermouth (which would have been sweet) and gin. The city of Martinez likes to lay claim to the invention of this drink, saying that a lucky miner who had struck gold in the Gold Rush was travelling back through Martinez and asked the bartender for Champagne; he didn't have any so mixed him up this delightful concoction and the miner took it on with him to San Francisco. A nice but completely unverifiable story! There are other bartenders with names such as Martini and Martine, who have claims, as does the theory that the Martini brand of vermouth was so ubiquitous that instead of asking for a gin and Martini, people just started asking for a Martini. Either way, by the late 1890s the Martinez had evolved with changing palates, and the arrival of new, dryer styles of gin, into the Dry Martini – most recipes called for equal parts gin and vermouth with orange bitters. During Prohibition the gin would have been low-quality 'bathtub' gin, with the vermouth there to disguise it. However, over the next few years and after Prohibition ended we see this Dry Martini drying out even further with bartenders using less and less vermouth, and the orange bitters falling out of fashion. The gin became the hero, to the point that Winston Churchill reportedly took his Martini as ice-cold gin with a bow in the direction of France.

The Martini is almost infinitely personalisable, to the point that it feels redundant to actually give a recipe. I'm a 'there's a Martini for every occasion' kind of a person, but some people like to have a failsafe signature. It is a drink that I often see people struggle to order at the bar, as they're not sure what the terms mean.

1. *Pick your spirit*
   The Martini was originally gin, but we're not puritans here so if vodka is your thing then do it. Either way, make sure you choose a spirit with good texture.

2. *Decide how dry you like your Martini*
   'Dry', in this context, is not the opposite of 'sweet', but the opposite of 'wet', and this refers to the amount of vermouth used in the cocktail. While the perception in drinks culture is often 'the dryer the better', please don't be scared of a Wet Martini! It's a delicious drink, and especially good to make sure you're not on the floor before dinner.

3. *Choose your garnish*
   A lot of people like a Dirty Martini, which adds a dash of olive brine to the actual drink as well as olives, or you can just have your Martini garnished with olives (because who doesn't love a snack with their cocktail). In a similar vein, the Gibson Martini is garnished with a pickled onion. If savoury isn't your thing, go for a citrus zest twist (see page 75). Lemon is the go-to here, but some gins taste really good with a grapefruit or an orange zest twist depending on their botanicals. There are boundless additions to be played with – a dash of dry sherry or absinthe, or even a rinse of smoky scotch.

4. *Make sure everything is very cold*
   It's ideal if you can keep your spirit and glass in the freezer for a really viscous texture, but if not, make sure you stir on the best ice possible until it feels icy cold. Serve in a coupe or Martini glass.

THE JABBERWOCKY

This drink is a modern adaptation of the Jabberwock from *The Savoy Cocktail Book* and is sophisticated and complex, yet still light. It's my go-to nightcap in the summer months. It may not be a strict Martini, but definitely falls in the same category to me!

INGREDIENTS

20 ml (⅔ oz) gin

20 ml (⅔ oz) manzanilla sherry

20 ml (⅔ oz) Lillet Blanc or other white vermouth

2 dashes orange bitters

Served up (no ice)

Garnish: lemon zest twist (see page 75)

EQUIPMENT

Glassware: coupe or Martini glass

Mixing glass

Jigger

Bar spoon

Julep strainer

METHOD

Add all the ingredients to a mixing glass and stir until chilled and diluted. Use the Julep strainer to hold the ice back in the mixing glass and pour into your chilled coupe glass. Fold your twist over the top to expel the oils, then use as a garnish.

Gin
Dry Sherry
Vermouth
Bitters

THE FAMOUS ONE

THE NEGRONI

As with almost every classic cocktail that has been around for a while, the origins of the Negroni are somewhat disputed. The story goes that the Negroni is an evolution of the Americano, which in itself is an evolution of the Milano Torino. The Milano Torino is a super simple aperitif drink, made from equal parts Campari (from Milan) and sweet vermouth (from Turin), and has been around since the 1860s. When Americans started arriving on the scene for holidays around the time of Prohibition, they liked the drink but, being used to Highballs, asked for it with a splash of soda water (club soda) – hence, the Americano. The next bit is the best, but not necessarily accurate, story. There was a Count Camillo Negroni, who was a bit of a wild child, and he asked his local in Florence for something like an Americano, but stronger. The bartender substituted gin for soda water, and the rest is history . . . but quite widely contested history. The first printed recipes for Negronis started appearing in the late 1940s but there were definitely similar and identical recipes appearing as early as the 1920s under different names.

INGREDIENTS

30 ml (1 oz) gin

30 ml (1 oz) Campari

30 ml (1 oz) sweet vermouth

Ice: large block

Garnish: orange zest twist
(see page 75)

EQUIPMENT

Glassware: rocks glass

Jigger

Mixing glass

Julep strainer

Bar spoon

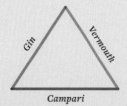

METHOD

Add all the ingredients to your mixing glass and stir until desired dilution. Use the Julep strainer to hold the ice back in the mixing glass and pour into your chilled rocks glass. Fold your twist over the top to expel the oils, then use as a garnish.

Pro Tip:
The Negroni was always a café drink, it was never meant to be fancy. So, while you can do it 'properly' in a mixing glass and over block ice, this is a favourite of mine to prebatch and pour out at parties over whatever ice you have available, with a (clean!) finger-stir and a wedge of orange. When doing this I like to use more vermouth and less gin to keep it lower in alcohol, and call it a Party Negroni!

THE WHITE NEGRONI

Many bartenders have riffed on the Negroni's simple formula. One of the most successful versions is the White Negroni. It was invented in 2001 by a British bartender named Wayne Collins. He had travelled to France for a cocktail competition and had a hankering for a Negroni. Being in a different country he decided to take advantage of French ingredients, creating this summery and herbal riff. This idea of substituting in local ingredients works really well, especially in Australia where we produce great gin, vermouth and bitters.

INGREDIENTS

Ingredients Note:
[1] *The original was Lillet Blanc but most white vermouths work.*

40 ml (1⅓ oz) gin

30 ml (1 oz) white vermouth[1]

20 ml (⅔ oz) Suze

Ice: large block

Garnish: grapefruit zest twist (see page 75)

EQUIPMENT

Glassware: rocks glass

Jigger

Mixing glass

Julep strainer

Bar spoon

METHOD

Add all the ingredients to your mixing glass and stir until desired dilution. Use the Julep strainer to hold the ice back in the mixing glass and pour into your chilled rocks glass. Fold your twist over the top to expel the oils, then use as a garnish.

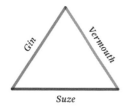

⌣

CARIÑO

This is a Negroni twist I make for a more dessert-style take on the bittersweet blueprint. It had remained nameless until I featured it in a video, when the Cariño was suggested as merging my name and one of the ingredients – plus it means 'affection' in Spanish, which is definitely how I feel about Negroni variations in general!

INGREDIENTS

Ingredients Note:
[1] I use a local cacao and nut bitters, but Angostura would work as well.

30 ml (1 oz) aged rum

30 ml (1 oz) Amaro Nonino

30 ml (1 oz) Cocchi Americano

2 dashes bitters[1]

Ice: large block

Garnish: orange zest twist (see page 75)

EQUIPMENT

Glassware: rocks glass

Jigger

Mixing glass

Julep strainer

Bar spoon

METHOD

Add all the ingredients to a mixing glass and stir until desired dilution. Use the Julep strainer to hold the ice back in the mixing glass and pour into your chilled rocks glass. Fold your twist over the top to expel the oils, then use as a garnish.

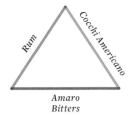

Rum · Cocchi Americano · Amaro Bitters

CITRUSY
AND FRESH

While the Old Fashioned and friends might be the original 'cocktail', Punches were being drunk well before the word cocktail actually existed. While coming in many different formulations, Punches contain strong (a spirit of some kind), sweet, weak (some kind of dilution, often water or tea) and, importantly, sour. The cocktails in this chapter can be thought of as individualised versions of that template, relying on the all-important citrus for zing and balance. Switching out the sweet element in these drinks for different syrups and liqueurs is an easy way to start experimenting with flavours yourself!

Low and No:

Non-alcoholic spirit replacements come into their own in these drinks – the citrus and syrups provide enough other flavours that you might not even notice you're not drinking the real deal! A citrus oleo is a good replacement for orange liqueurs as it brings a bit of bitterness from the peels, which helps add structure.

THE DAIQUIRI

Mixing rum with citrus was nothing new – it saved many a sailor from scurvy from as early as the 1600s. The Daiquiri as we now know it has a fairly well-substantiated history. In the late 1800s, the USA started mining in Cuba, and one such venture was headed by a gentleman named Jennings Cox. Among other employment enticements was a monthly ration of the local rum, Bacardi. The story goes that Cox ran out of gin when entertaining guests so mixed his rum with some lime and sugar, and voila! It became popular with the other miners and, since they all worked together in the mines in Daiquiri, Cox decided to name it after the village. In turn, it was picked up by popular Cuban drinking establishments, such as El Floridita. It became synonymous with Cuban drinking culture, which was massively romanticised in the US at the beginning of the 20th century (notably by Ernest Hemingway), and so the Daiquiri made its way Stateside and into the classic cocktail hall of fame, where it remains to this day.

Pro Tip: COLD IS KEY!
Melbourne bartender extraordinaire, Nathan Beasley, has been known to say 'the Daiquiri is the bartender's answer to air conditioning, so it has to be bracingly cold', and I couldn't agree more. If you can, keep your glass in the freezer and, while you should always shake hard, this time shake REALLY REALLY HARD! The original recipe actually called for both water and ice, so dilution is really important here. Some bartenders will shake on a mixture of crushed and cubed ice. I tend to just use cubed ice, but shake a little longer than usual, until the tin is really good and frosty.

For this reason as well, some people prefer to single-strain a Daiquiri so there are still some little ice shards floating in there. I go the middle road, and use a Julep strainer rather than a fine strainer for my second strain – it removes any big chunks of ice while allowing a few through for that icy, refreshing effect.

$>$

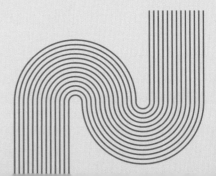

The simple combination of lime, sugar and white rum has stood the test of time, and a good Daiquiri is seen as a badge of honour amongst bartenders as it is so simple but so easy to screw up! I'm going to show you how to master the balance of these three ingredients and you'll be transporting you and your pals to sunny Cuba in no time.

INGREDIENTS

60 ml (2 oz) white rum[1]

20 ml (⅔ oz) fresh lime juice

10 ml (⅓ oz) cane sugar syrup (see page 44)

Strip of lime zest

Served up (no ice)

EQUIPMENT

Glassware: chilled coupe or Martini glass

Jigger

Shaker tin

Hawthorne strainer

Julep strainer

A vegetable peeler

Ingredients Note:
[1]Any light, grassy and fruity white rum will work for a classic Daiquiri, but don't be afraid to experiment with a spiced rum or a big and funky rum for a bolder take.

METHOD

A Note on Ratio:
You may notice the proportions are slightly different than my usual 2:1:½. You really want the rum to shine through in this one, and this 3:1:½ formula makes a Daiquiri Hemingway would be proud of. Usual sour proportions definitely work as well, it will just be a much more citrus forward drink.

Using your vegetable peeler, cut a small strip of lime zest with as little pith as possible (you want the aromatic oils but not too much bitterness). Squeeze your lime and add all of the ingredients to your shaker tin. Add ice and shake hard. Use your Hawthorne strainer to hold the ice back in the tin and pour through the Julep strainer into an ice cold glass. No need to garnish – this drink is simplicity itself!

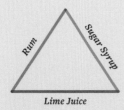

Rum Sugar Syrup

Lime Juice

THE HEMINGWAY DAIQUIRI

Hemingway was a well-known bon vivant, so it is unsurprising he has a cocktail named after him! Allegedly, he was using the toilet at Havana's legendary El Floridita bar when he saw them serving up frozen Daiquiris. He tried one and declared it passable, but that he would prefer it with no sugar and double the rum. Understandably, normal people didn't find the straight rum and lime blend quite as palatable as Hemingway did, so El Floridita tweaked it a little, using maraschino liqueur for a hint of sweetness and grapefruit juice to soften the lime, while still being nice and tart.

Ingredients Note:
[1] *I like using Cuban rum as a nod to the cocktail's birthplace, but any light and fruity white rum works well.*

INGREDIENTS

60 ml (2 oz) white rum[1]

15 ml (½ oz) fresh lime juice

15 ml (½ oz) grapefruit juice

10 ml (⅓ oz) maraschino liqueur

5 ml (⅙ oz) sugar syrup (see page 44)

Served up (no ice)

Garnish: grapefruit zest twist (see page 81) and a maraschino cherry

EQUIPMENT

Glassware: coupe or Martini glass

Jigger

Shaker tin

Hawthorne strainer

Fine strainer

Rum · Lime Juice · Grapefruit Juice

Maraschino
Sugar Syrup

METHOD

Add all of the ingredients to your shaker tin and shake as hard as you can! Double-strain into a chilled coupe. Fold your grapefruit zest over the top of the drink to release the oils, then discard. Drop a maraschino cherry in for garnish.

⌣

THE ROYAL BERMUDA YACHT CLUB

A Trader Vic (Victor Bergeron) creation, this tropical Daiquiri twist shows how switching out one or two ingredients can really transform a cocktail!

Ingredients Notes:
[1] *I actually prefer a full-bodied white rum to keep it brighter and fruitier, but the original recipe is made with an aged rum, which gives a richer cocktail.*

[2] *Falernum is a nut and spice-based syrup that is often used in tropical drinks – its ginger, lime, cinnamon and clove notes go so well with rum. You can make it yourself, or there are several good-quality commercial ones on the market.*

INGREDIENTS

50 ml (1⅔ oz) rum[1]

20 ml (⅔ oz) fresh lime juice

10 ml (⅓ oz) falernum syrup[2]

10 ml (⅓ oz) curaçao or other orange liqueur

Served up (no ice)

Garnish: lime wheel

EQUIPMENT

Glassware: coupe or Martini glass

Jigger

Shaker tin

Hawthorne strainer

Fine strainer

METHOD

Add all the ingredients to your shaker tin and shake as hard as you can! Double-strain into a chilled coupe and garnish with a lime wheel.

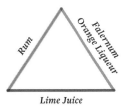

Rum — Falernum / Orange Liqueur

Lime Juice

CORPSE REVIVER NO.2

Bartenders are not known for their small egos, and the Corpse Reviver family is the result of them playing, if not God, at least doctors! These drinks emerged in the 1800s with mentions in fashionable publications such as *Punch* magazine. A few recipes appear under this name in cocktail books around this time, all of them wildly different, which leads me to believe that many bartenders would have had their own 'Corpse Reviver' that they swore by to loyal clientele. The man who made it stick, though, is Harry Craddock – arguably one of the most famous bartenders of all time. He was an Englishman who honed his craft in America, before returning to England when Prohibition hit (legend has it that he mixed the last legal drink in the US, but I have no idea how you would verify that!) to take the helm at the Savoy's legendary American Bar. It was here that he published *The Savoy Cocktail Book*, which is definitely still a worthwhile investment for anyone interested in cocktail culture. Not only are there seminal recipes, such as the Corpse Reviver No. 2 and the White Lady, but witty observations, such as my favourite about the former: 'Four of these taken in swift succession will unrevive the corpse again'.

Pro Tip:
The easiest way to achieve the 'rinse' is to find a little atomiser like the kind used for perfume. They're usually pretty easily found at dollar store establishments, and you can fill them with absinthe and squirt directly into your glass. If you don't have an atomiser, just pop a little dribble (5–10 ml/⅙–⅓ oz) into your glass and swirl it around, trying to get as close to the rim of the glass as possible, then discard the rest of the absinthe.

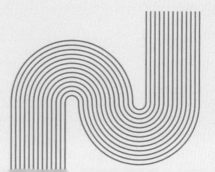

INGREDIENTS

20 ml (⅔ oz) gin

20 ml (⅔ oz) Cocchi Americano or Lillet Blanc[1]

20 ml (⅔ oz) curaçao or other orange liqueur

20 ml (⅔ oz) fresh lemon juice

Absinthe, to rinse

Served up (no ice)

Garnish: lemon zest twist (see page 81; optional)

Ingredients Note:
[1] *Harry Craddock's recipe called for Kina Lillet, which is no longer made. Kina Lillet had more quinine in it (similar to Cocchi) so, if substituting in another white vermouth, try to find one that has quite a pronounced bitterness, or add a dash of orange bitters.*

EQUIPMENT

Glassware: coupe or Martini glass

Jigger

Shaker tin

Hawthorne strainer

Fine strainer

An atomiser

METHOD

Add all the ingredients, except the absinthe, to your shaker tin. Fill with ice and shake hard! Spritz your chilled coupe with absinthe and double-strain the cocktail into the glass. Fold your twist over the top to expel the oils, then use as a garnish.

Gin / Cocchi Americano / Orange Liqueur / Lemon Juice / Absinthe

SOUTHSIDE

A recipe that has been around in some form since 1916 (although then it was a Fizz, lengthened out with soda water/club soda), this short, sharp and minty concoction is a go-to when someone looks for a cocktail recommendation. Don't overdo it on the mint as it can become overpowering – I don't tend to muddle, just shake with the leaves in there. Adding cucumber in the shaker as well makes an Eastside, another fun twist!

Ingredients Note:
[1] The Southside Fizz recipe contained both lemon and lime juice so recipes tend to fluctuate between both. I like the sharpness of lime but either works!

INGREDIENTS

50 ml (1⅔ oz) gin

20 ml (⅔ oz) sugar syrup (see page 44)

20 ml (⅔ oz) fresh lime juice[1]

5 mint leaves

Served up (no ice)

Garnish: small mint sprig or a large mint leaf

EQUIPMENT

Glassware: coupe or Martini glass

Jigger

Shaker tin

Hawthorne strainer

Fine strainer

METHOD

Add all the ingredients to your shaker tin, add ice and shake hard. Double-strain (the fine straining is important here to make sure you don't end up with mint in your teeth!) into your chilled coupe and float the mint sprig or leaf on the surface.

Gin · Sugar Syrup · Lime Juice

LONDON CALLING

This drink was made in 2002 for a cocktail competition, so its history is not as rich as some we have looked at, but it has become a modern classic because of its delicious and complex flavours. It's also where we started to see modern bartenders' love affair with dry sherry in drinks.

Ingredients Note:
[1] *A navy-strength or overproof gin works well to give this cocktail the oomph it needs!*

INGREDIENTS

40 ml (1⅓ oz) gin[1]

15 ml (½ oz) fino sherry

15 ml (½ oz) fresh lemon juice

15 ml (½ oz) sugar syrup
(see page 44)

2 dashes orange bitters

Served up (no ice)

Garnish: grapefruit zest twist
(see page 81)

EQUIPMENT

Glassware: coupe or
Martini glass

Jigger

Shaker tin

Hawthorne strainer

Fine strainer

METHOD

Add all the ingredients to your shaker tin and shake. Double-strain into a chilled coupe. Fold your twist over the top to expel the oils, then use as a garnish.

Gin
Dry Sherry
Sugar Syrup
Lemon Juice

THE WHISKEY SOUR

When sailors returned to land after time at sea there were probably plenty of things they didn't miss, but they did miss their grog – rum rations mixed with citrus. No longer in the Caribbean, though, they would have substituted in whatever spirit was to hand. In the US, this meant whiskey! The Whiskey Sour began to be mentioned in newspaper articles in the 1870s – in fact, cocktail historian David Wondrich dug up a quote from the *Atlanta Daily Constitution*, which says, 'When American meets American then comes the Whiskey Sour', underlining how important it had become in the nation's drinking culture.

Ingredients Note:
[1] *You can of course make a Whiskey Sour with any whisk(e)y you like – in Australia, people actually often prefer scotch so I make a point of asking for a preference.*

INGREDIENTS

60 ml (2 oz) bourbon[1]

30 ml (1 oz) fresh lemon juice

15 ml (½ oz) sugar syrup (see page 44)

10–15 ml (⅓–½ oz) egg white

Ice: cube ice

Garnish: orange zest twist (see page 81) and a cherry (optional)

EQUIPMENT

Glassware: rocks glass

Jigger

Shaker tin

Hawthorne strainer

Fine strainer

METHOD

Add all the ingredients to your shaker tin, double-shake (once with and once without ice). Double-strain into your rocks glass. Fold your orange twist over the top to expel the oils, then garnish with the twist and a cherry.

Whiskey / Sugar Syrup / Lemon Juice

Pro Tip:

Original Whiskey Sour recipes did not contain egg white. The ingredient started popping up in recipes around 30 years after the drink was first popularised, and some argue it should technically be called a Boston Sour (but really, they should get a hobby!). These days I find that egg white and its resultant foamy texture is an expected part of the Whiskey Sour experience. For notes on double-shaking see page 78.

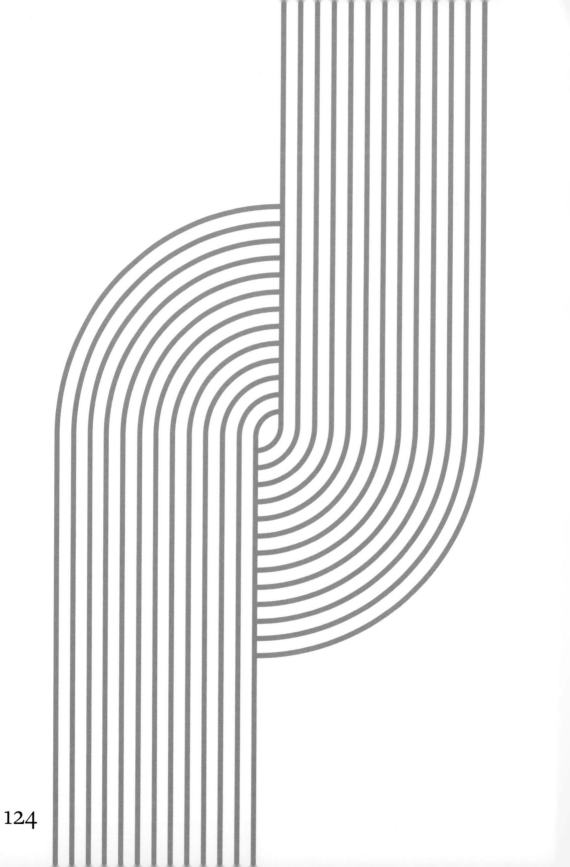

124

⌣

THE PENICILLIN

This drink is the brainchild of Sam Ross, an Australian bartender who has gone on to worldwide fame for his simple, yet genius, modern classics. This is essentially just a Scotch Sour, but using honey and ginger syrup and a little splash of smoky whisk(e)y layers in complexity and spice. It really will cure what ails you! Sam Ross also created the Paper Plane, an equal parts bourbon and amaro banger, which is definitely worth a look.

Ingredients Note:
[1] The easiest way to make this is to combine honey 1:1 with water and roughly chopped ginger (about 2.5 cm/ 1 inch per 100 ml/ 3 oz). Combine over a gentle heat, then allow to sit overnight before straining the ginger out. The longer you leave the ginger in, the spicier it will be!

INGREDIENTS

60 ml (2 oz) blended Scottish whisky

25 ml (¾ oz) honey and ginger syrup[1]

25 ml (¾ oz) fresh lemon juice

7.5 ml (¼ oz) peated whisky (most Islay malts are perfect)

Ice: cube ice

Garnish: candied ginger

EQUIPMENT

Glassware: rocks glass

Jigger

Shaker tin

Hawthorne strainer

Fine strainer

METHOD

Add all the ingredients, except the peated whisky, to your shaker tin, add ice and shake. Double-strain into your rocks glass. 'Float' the peated whisky on top by pouring over the back of a bar spoon. Skewer a piece of candied ginger and garnish.

Scotch — Honey and Ginger Syrup — Lemon Juice

⌣

SCOFFLAW

The name comes from a competition run by a Prohibitionist to coin
a word to describe those flauting the law and continuing to drink . . .
I don't think it achieved the effect they wanted it to! The drink, though,
is not American but French, albeit from Harry's New York Bar in Paris.

INGREDIENTS

50 ml (1⅔ oz) rye whiskey

25 ml (¾ oz) dry vermouth

15 ml (½ oz) fresh lemon juice

10 ml (⅓ oz) grenadine
(see page 47)

2 dashes orange bitters

Served up (no ice)

Garnish: lemon zest twist
(see page 75)

EQUIPMENT

Glassware: coupe or
Martini glass

Jigger

Shaker tin

Hawthorne strainer

Fine strainer

METHOD

Add all the ingredients to your shaker tin and shake. Double-strain into
a chilled coupe. Fold your lemon twist over the top to expel the oils, then
use as a garnish.

Whiskey / Grenadine / Dry Vermouth / Bitters / Lemon Juice

THE SIDECAR

The Sidecar's exact birthplace is debated, but it's safe to say it gained notoriety after World War 1 at Harry's New York Bar in Paris and was inducted into the cocktail hall of fame with its inclusion in the seminal bartending book by the same Harry: *Harry's ABC of Mixing Cocktails*. The name of the cocktail is also disputed – some say it was named after an army captain who used to arrive at the bar in a motorcycle sidecar; others say it comes from the bartending practice of pouring any excess cocktail from the shaker into a little shot glass to the side once the cocktail glass was full.

INGREDIENTS

50 ml (1⅔ oz) brandy

20 ml (⅔ oz) fresh lemon juice

20 ml (⅔ oz) curaçao or other orange liqueur

Garnish: half a granulated sugar rim and a lemon zest twist (see page 75)

Served up (no ice)

EQUIPMENT

Glassware: coupe or Martini glass

Jigger

Shaker tin

Hawthorne strainer

Fine strainer

METHOD

Run a lemon wedge around the outside of half of the glass and dab in sugar, shaking off any excess. Add all the ingredients to your shaker tin, add as much ice as will fit and shake hard. Double-strain into your chilled and rimmed glass. Fold your lemon twist over the top to expel the oils, then discard.

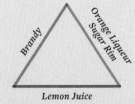

128

JACK ROSE

An origin story involving a New York gangster and an appearance in a Hemingway novel helps to lend some pretty serious street cred to this unassuming pink drink – even if the gangster story is probably untrue! The drink was actually already quite popular before the gambler Bald Jack Rose gained notoriety in a 1912 murder case. The apple and pomegranate (from the grenadine) combination here makes a delicious, warm Sour.

INGREDIENTS

50 ml (1⅔ oz) applejack or other apple brandy

20 ml (⅔ oz) grenadine (see page 47)

20 ml (⅔ oz) fresh lime juice

Served up (no ice)

Garnish: dehydrated apple slice (optional)

EQUIPMENT

Glassware: coupe or Martini glass

Jigger

Shaker tin

Hawthorne strainer

Fine strainer

METHOD

Add all the ingredients to your shaker tin, fill with ice and shake as hard as you can. Double-strain into your chilled coupe glass. Float your dehydrated apple slice on the surface, if using.

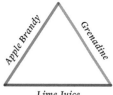

‿

CHARLIE CHAPLIN

Created at the Waldorf Astoria, this fruity Sour is as much of a crowd pleaser as its namesake.

A Note on Ratio:
Because the apricot brandy and sloe gins here both form the strong and the sweet elements of this cocktail, the equal parts ratio actually works perfectly.

INGREDIENTS

30 ml (1 oz) apricot brandy

30 ml (1 oz) sloe gin

30 ml (1 oz) fresh lime juice

Served up (no ice)

Garnish: dehydrated lime wheel (optional)

EQUIPMENT

Glassware: coupe or Martini glass

Jigger

Shaker tin

Hawthorne strainer

Fine strainer

METHOD

Add all the ingredients to your shaker tin, fill with ice and shake as hard as you can. Double-strain into your chilled coupe glass. Float your dehydrated lime wheel on the surface, if using.

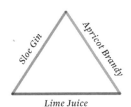

Sloe Gin / Apricot Brandy / Lime Juice

THE MARGARITA

Of course such an iconic drink is going to have a few glitzy origin stories. There are claims that it was named after a Spanish dancer who was allergic to all spirits except tequila; another story is that it was named after Rita Hayworth (whose real name was Margarita). What's much more likely is that it is simply a Spanish translation of Daisy, a class of cocktails very popular around the time the Margarita came on the scene in the 1930s. Daisies are essentially Sours (so always contain citrus), but with a liqueur or flavoured syrup as the sweetener rather than just sugar syrup, and are generally topped up with soda water (club soda). That tourists might have made their way across the southern US border and requested a Daisy, and an obliging Mexican bartender mixed one up for them with tequila is not hard to imagine!

INGREDIENTS

60 ml (2 oz) blanco tequila

30 ml (1 oz) fresh lime juice

15 ml (½ oz) curaçao or other orange liqueur

Served up (no ice)

Garnish: salt rim

EQUIPMENT

Glassware: coupe or Martini glass

Jigger

Shaker tin

Hawthorne strainer

Fine strainer

METHOD

Use a lime wedge to wet the edge of your glass and dab in salt, shaking off any excess. Add all the ingredients to your shaker tin and shake. Double-strain into a chilled coupe.

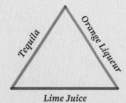

Pro Tip:
While a salt rim is non-negotiable, I like to only rim half the glass so that the drinker can control how much or how little to take in with each sip. See page 77 for the perfect technique.

TOMMY'S MARGARITA

This is the bartender's Margarita. Invented by Julio Bermejo at his family's restaurant in California, where the cocktail gets its name, he simply switches out the orange liqueur for agave syrup. This natural sweetener is made from the same plant as the spirit, which makes for a perfectly harmonious floral flavour profile. It is served on the rocks, so lasts a little longer on a hot day, and Julio forgoes the salt rim to let the tequila really shine. I personally feel a bit cheated without one, so I like to do half a salt rim and give people the choice!

INGREDIENTS

Ingredients Note:
[1] *I also love this drink made with mezcal.*

60 ml (2 oz) blanco tequila[1]

30 ml (1 oz) fresh lime juice

15 ml (½ oz) agave syrup

Ice: cube ice

Garnish: salt rim (optional)

EQUIPMENT

Glassware: rocks glass

Jigger

Shaker tin

Hawthorne strainer

METHOD

Use a lime wedge to wet the edge of your glass and dab in salt, shaking off any excess. Add all the ingredients to your shaker tin and shake. Strain into your rocks glass (fine-straining isn't necessary as you're serving on ice anyway, so little ice chips aren't a problem!).

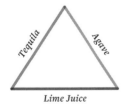

Tequila   Agave

Lime Juice

THE TOREADOR

The Toreador actually predates the famous Margarita – it first appeared in the *Café Royale Cocktail Book* in 1937, when tequila was relatively unheard of outside of Mexico. I actually find it an easier introduction to tequila than the punchy Margarita as it is smoother and fruitier, but definitely packs enough agave punch to satisfy ardent Margarita drinkers looking to mix things up!

Ingredients Notes:
[1] I like to use a fruity bitters like fig and cinnamon if you have something similar, otherwise Angostura works great!

[2] This is sometimes necessary to balance depending on your brand of apricot brandy – taste before adding.

INGREDIENTS

50 ml (1⅔ oz) blanco tequila

20 ml (⅔ oz) apricot brandy

20 ml (⅔ oz) fresh lime juice

1 dash bitters[1]

5 ml (⅙ oz) sugar syrup[2] (see page 44)

Served up (no ice)

Garnish: dehydrated lime wheel or none

EQUIPMENT

Glassware: coupe or Martini glass

Jigger

Shaker tin

Hawthorne strainer

Fine strainer

METHOD

Add all the ingredients to your shaker tin and shake. Double-strain into a chilled coupe. Garnish with a dehydrated lime wheel, if using.

Tequila

Apricot Brandy

Lime Juice Bitters

TALL AND REFRESHING

Fizzes, Spritzes . . . even the names of these drinks evoke refreshment.
Their common feature is that they are lengthened out with something
bubbly – unlike the previous two chapters where the libations are short
and punchy, these are effervescent and lighter, well-suited to a sunny
afternoon. They are generally fairly simple, with the strong, sweet and
sour elements being quite obvious, and the lengthening out making them
easier to balance than some other styles of drinks, so they are great for
beginner bartenders. They are also good ones to add fresh fruit and herbs
to – garnishing a Tom Collins with sage or adding some fresh raspberries
to a Mojito will never go amiss.

Ingredients Note:

*A lot of the drinks in this chapter are 'topped' with a mixer. I haven't
included precise measurements because a little variation is fine (somewhere
between 60 ml/2 oz and 90 ml/3 oz is generally good), but if you're using
very large glassware you'll want to scale the whole drink up so all the
other flavours don't get drowned out.*

Low and No:

*These drinks work really well as non-alcoholic options – you can usually
just leave out the booze and they're still delicious! Substituting in shrubs as
the base works well too – they introduce different flavours without making
the drink too sweet. Teas are a good way to introduce structure as they have
tannin, either by making a tea syrup or using chilled tea to lengthen out the
drink. Or, use dry sherry or vermouth as the base for a low-alcohol option –
see the Rebujito, for example (page 141).*

THE FAMOUS ONE

THE TOM COLLINS

It seems likely that the Tom Collins evolved from the Gin Punch, perhaps helped along by John Collins who was a bartender at Limmer's Hotel in London, which was renowned for its Gin Punch. The drink was usually originally made using Old Tom gin, a sweeter, heavier style of gin that predates London Dry gin. But what's the difference between this and a Gin Fizz? Well, when it comes to a regular Gin Fizz and a Tom Collins, not much to be honest! But David Wondrich has made the distinction that Collinses are built and served on ice with plenty of soda water (club soda), whereas Fizzes are shaken and served shorter, not on ice – hence why you can have variations, such as the Silver Fizz, which contains egg.

Pro Tip:
For all drinks that are topped up, I prefer to add the mixer before the ice, to around halfway up the glass. This keeps them more consistent.

INGREDIENTS

60 ml (2 oz) gin

30 ml (1 oz) fresh lemon juice

15 ml (½ oz) sugar syrup (see page 44)

Soda water (club soda) to top (around 90 ml/3 oz)

Ice: cube ice

Garnish: lemon wheels and a cherry

EQUIPMENT

Glassware: Highball

Jigger

Bar spoon

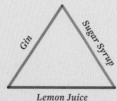

METHOD

Add all the ingredients to your glass. Add ice and stir. Garnish with lemon wheels suspended throughout the drink and a skewered cherry and lemon wheel on top.

138

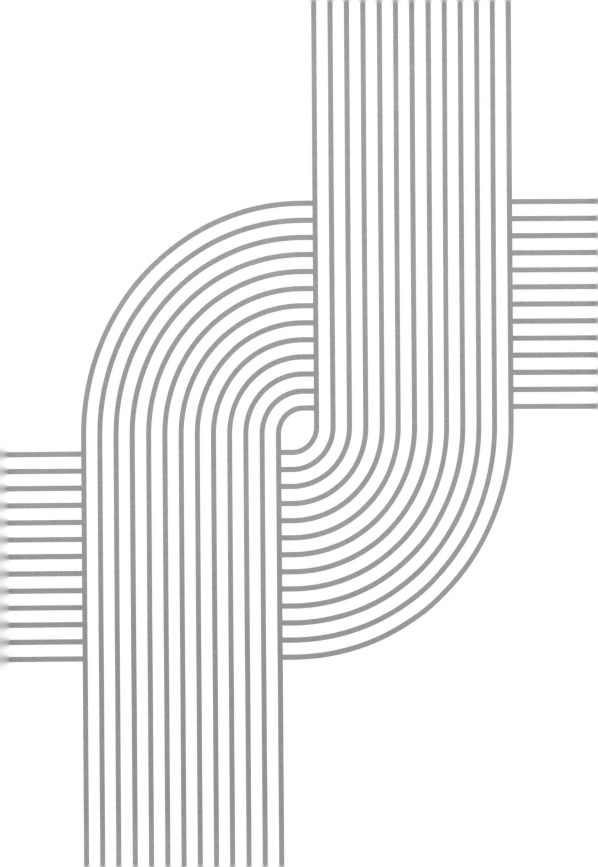

THE PALOMA

Some flavour combinations are just meant to be and tequila and grapefruit is a match made in heaven. It has been around since the 1950s and, while not a Collins by name, it's certainly a Collins by nature – tall, tart and thirst quenching.

Ingredients Notes:
[1] *Blanco tequila works best for a crisp and clean Paloma, but a reposado can add a nice richness.*

[2] *I find this adds a nice balance and richness, but is optional.*

[3] *Grapefruit soda is traditional and there are lots of good-quality ones on the market now, but you can embrace the fresh and squeeze 45 ml (1½ oz) fresh grapefruit juice and top with regular soda water (club soda).*

INGREDIENTS

60 ml (2 oz) blanco tequila[1]

15 ml (½ oz) fresh lime juice

5 ml (⅙ oz) agave syrup[2]

Grapefruit soda to top[3]

Ice: cube ice

Garnish: salt rim (optional) and a lime wheel

EQUIPMENT

Glassware: Highball glass

Jigger

Bar spoon

METHOD

If doing a salt rim, use a lime wedge to wet the edge of your glass and dab in salt, shaking off any excess. Add the rest of the ingredients to your glass, add ice and stir. Garnish with a lime wheel.

Tequila

Agave

Lime Juice
Grapefruit Soda

140

⌣

THE REBUJITO

The Rebujito's exact origins are unknown – whether its inspiration owes more to the Sherry Cobbler or the Highball family is up for (fairly redundant) debate, but either way it seems to have been invented for Seville's La Feria de Abril. Week-long festivities with constant toasting in the heat call for something low in alcohol and high in refreshment and, when you're a hop, skip and a jump from the Sherry Triangle, it's a pretty obvious move to build around the distinctively flavoured wine of the region.

Ingredients Note:
[1] *The lightest of the sherries are the traditional, but sometimes I like to use a richer amontillado or oloroso and pair with a mandarin oleo.*

INGREDIENTS

60 ml (2 oz) fino or manzanilla sherry[1]

15 ml (½ oz) fresh lemon juice

15 ml (½ oz) fresh lime juice

20 ml (⅔ oz) sugar syrup (see page 44)

Top with soda water (club soda)

Ice: cube ice

Garnish: lemon wheels and a mint sprig

EQUIPMENT

Glassware: Highball glass

Jigger

Bar spoon

METHOD

Add all the ingredients to your glass. Add ice and stir. Garnish with lemon wheels suspended throughout the drink and a mint sprig on top.

Dry Sherry / Sugar Syrup / Lemon Juice Lime Juice

THE MOSCOW MULE

Imagine a time when vodka was not ubiquitous – the Moscow Mule is the success of one of the first viral marketing campaigns. A struggling vodka salesman and a bar owner with a surplus of homemade ginger beer joined forces. They made use of the recently invented Polaroid camera to take pictures of bartenders and guests with a bottle of the vodka and their Moscow Mule served in the deliciously frosty copper mug, and used these to build up the credibility of the brand and the drink.

INGREDIENTS

Ingredients Note:
[1] Make sure you get a good, spicy one – it really makes the drink.

60 ml (2 oz) vodka

20 ml (⅔ oz) fresh lime juice

Top with ginger beer[1]

Ice: cube ice

Garnish: lime wheel

EQUIPMENT

Glassware: copper mug or Highball glass

Jigger

Bar spoon

METHOD

Add all the ingredients to your glass. Add ice and stir. Garnish with a lime wheel.

DARK 'N' STORMY

Unsurprisingly for a rum cocktail, this drink was apparently a naval invention – the Royal Navy was making ginger beer on Bermuda, where there is also a rum distillery, and it wasn't long before the sailors thought to combine the two!

INGREDIENTS

Ingredients Notes:
[1] The chewier the better for this one in my opinion – a big, funky, molasses-based rum is ideal.

[2] Make sure you get a good, spicy one – it really makes the drink.

60 ml (2 oz) aged rum[1]

30 ml (1 oz) fresh lime juice

Top with ginger beer[2]

3 dashes Angostura bitters

Ice: cube ice

Garnish: lime wheels

EQUIPMENT

Glassware: Highball glass

Jigger

Bar spoon

METHOD

Add all the ingredients, except the bitters, to your glass. Add the ice and stir. Dash the bitters on top to form a float. Garnish with lime wheels suspended through the drink.

Rum — Ginger Beer

Lime Juice
Bitters

EL DIABLO

Credited to Trader Vic, the El Diablo is fiery and punchy – it lives up to its name! We've seen blanco tequila work well with stone fruits and citrus, but the richness of a reposado tequila works so well with berries.

Pro Tip:
While you can absolutely just build this drink, I prefer to lighten the syrupy texture of the cassis by shaking first, but I do like to hold back a little cassis to float for aesthetic effect.

Ingredients Note:
[1] Make sure you get a good, spicy one – it really makes the drink.

INGREDIENTS

45 ml (1½ oz) reposado tequila

15 ml (½ oz) fresh lime juice

Top with ginger beer[1]

15 ml (½ oz) crème de cassis

Ice: cube ice

Garnish: lime wheel

EQUIPMENT

Glassware: Highball glass

Jigger

Shaker tin

Hawthorne strainer

Bar spoon

METHOD

Add all the ingredients, except the ginger beer and 5 ml (⅙ oz) of cassis to your shaker tin. Add ice and shake. Strain into your Highball glass, top with ginger beer and add fresh ice. Drizzle the excess cassis over the top of your bar spoon to create a float. Garnish with a lime wheel.

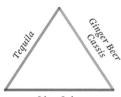

THE MOJITO

Warning: The Mojito Effect is a well-documented phenomenon among bartenders – as soon as you send one out, 10 more get ordered!

There are, as with all older cocktails, competing origin stories for the Mojito. The precursor to rum was called aguardiente de caña and was a really rough spirit – we're talking molasses moonshine here! Cubans would mix it with sugarcane juice, lime and mint – which were all readily available – to make it palatable. Along came Francis Drake to pillage Havana, but his crew were riddled with dysentery and scurvy. They sent some folks ashore looking for help and returned with this concoction (which I do think says a lot about the hospitable nature of islanders – I'd have been hoping the aguardiente turned them all blind). Instead, this magical tonic cured the crew, and Drake left having only fired a few shots. The drink became known as 'El Draque'. There are some other stories around Drake himself inventing the drink, but I think we should give credit to the Cubans!

The modern Mojito took form as lighter, refined rums entered the market and thirsty Americans overran Havana during Prohibition – it makes sense that they would look for the local equivalent to their beloved Julep! The name 'Mojito' also has a few possible explanations – some say it comes from the African 'mojo' meaning to cast a little spell, as a crude version would have been a knock-off drink for African workers on the sugar plantations. Others think it comes from the limey mojo seasoning, or from the Spanish mojar meaning 'wetness'. They all make sense to me as this drink is certainly limey, wet and magical!

Pro Tip:
A lot of recipes will tell you to muddle the lime and mint. Honestly, I like to keep this drink as light and crisp as possible – if I want something with a more intense flavour pop I'll have a Daiquiri or a Southside. I just give the mint a gentle clap to release the aromas and pop it in, and use freshly squeezed lime juice rather than wedges. Of course if you prefer to muddle, then go ahead – just try and be fairly gentle so you don't start extracting too much bitterness.

INGREDIENTS

60 ml (2 oz) white rum[1]

20 ml (⅔ oz) fresh lime juice

20 ml (⅔ oz) sugar syrup
(see page 44)

6–8 mint leaves

Top with soda water (club soda;
optional)[2]

Ice: crushed

Garnish: mint sprig

Ingredients Notes:
[1] Keep it light
and crisp.

[2] Nothing ruins a
Mojito more quickly
than drowning it in
soda water. Once I've
churned through with
ice, there is usually
only around 30 ml
(1 oz) worth of space
to add a splash of soda,
so you get a spritzy
first sip.

EQUIPMENT

Glassware: Highball glass

Tea towel (dish towel)

Mallet or rolling pin

Jigger

Bar spoon

METHOD

Of course this drink is much easier if you have access to a crushed ice machine! If not, take out some frustrations by wrapping cube ice in a tea towel and bashing with a mallet or rolling pin. I'll often recommend a 'shake and dump' technique (see page 182) to mimic the effect of crushed ice but, if you choose to do this here, I would add the mint after shaking.

Add all the ingredients, except the soda, to your glass and add crushed ice. Use your bar spoon to 'churn' or mix through thoroughly, suspending the mint leaves through the drink. Top with a splash of soda and garnish with a mint sprig.

Rum · Sugar Syrup · Lime Juice

148

GIN GIN MULE

Audrey Saunders is an icon of the cocktail renaissance we're currently experiencing and has created many a modern classic, including this one. If you cross a Mojito with a Moscow Mule and use gin, it's always going to be a crowd pleaser.

Ingredients Note:
[1] Audrey Saunders used a homemade ginger beer, which you can absolutely do – her recipe is available online. Because this is sharper she also uses a full 30 ml (1 oz) of sugar syrup, but this is too sweet if using a commercial ginger beer.

INGREDIENTS

1 mint sprig

20 ml (⅔ oz) sugar syrup (see page 44)

50 ml (1⅔ oz) gin

25 ml (¾ oz) fresh lime juice

30 ml (1 oz) ginger beer[1]

Ice: cube ice

Garnish: mint sprig

EQUIPMENT

Glassware: Highball glass

Jigger

Shaker tin

Muddler

Hawthorne strainer

Fine strainer

METHOD

Gently muddle one mint sprig in the sugar syrup. Add the other ingredients, except the ginger beer, then add ice and shake. Double-strain into a Highball glass and add the ginger beer and fresh ice. Garnish with another mint sprig.

THE UPPER EAST SIDE

I'm honestly not too sure who to credit this one to but I've picked it up somewhere along the way! An Eastside is a Southside (see page 120) with cucumber added and an Upper Eastside just adds soda water (club soda) too!

INGREDIENTS

2 cucumber ribbons (see method)

50 ml (1⅔ oz) gin

20 ml (⅔ oz) sugar syrup (see page 44)

20 ml (⅔ oz) fresh lime juice

5 mint leaves

Top with soda water (club soda)

Ice: cube ice

Garnish: mint sprig and cucumber ribbon (see page 76)

EQUIPMENT

Glassware: Highball glass

Vegetable peeler

Jigger

Bar spoon

METHOD

Use a vegetable peeler down the length of a cucumber to peel long ribbons. Twist two around the inside of your glass and roll one up for garnish. Add the ingredients to the Highball glass and fill with soda to around halfway. Add ice and garnish with a mint sprig and the rolled cucumber.

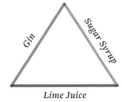

Gin | Sugar Syrup | Lime Juice

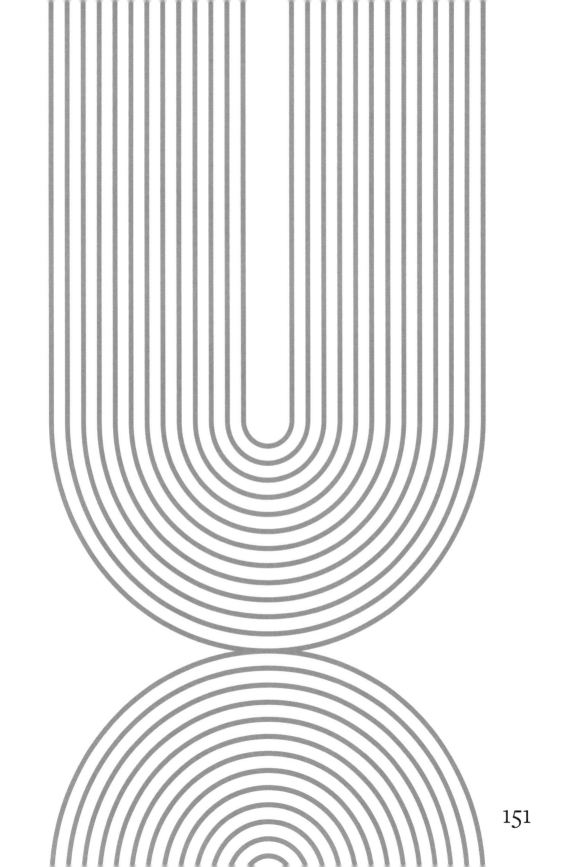

151

THE FAMOUS ONE

THE APEROL SPRITZ

The term 'Spritz' has been around for a very long time, and comes from the German for 'splash'. The story goes that Italian wines were too strong for refined Austro-Hungarian palates, so they would add a splash of soda water (club soda) to their white wines while they were busy occupying Northern Italy in the 19th century. In the 20th century, the Spritz as we know it – sparkling wine, Italian bitters and a splash of soda water – came to be. Lots of amari make a great Spritz so you can absolutely switch out the Aperol for another.

INGREDIENTS

60 ml (2 oz) Aperol

90 ml (3 oz) dry sparkling wine

30 ml (1 oz) soda water (club soda)

Ice: cubed ice

Garnish: a skewered olive (optional) and an orange wedge

EQUIPMENT

Glassware: wine glass

Jigger

Bar spoon

METHOD

Add all the ingredients to your glass. Add ice and stir. Garnish with an olive and an orange wedge.

THE AMERICANO

The spritzy forebear of the Negroni lengthens out the bittersweet flavours of Italy with a splash of soda water (club soda). It was first served in the 1860s at Caffè Campari in Milan, by Gaspare Campari who was experimenting with vehicles for his eponymous bitter. In my opinion, it's the ultimate aperitif!

INGREDIENTS

30 ml (1 oz) Campari

30 ml (1 oz) sweet vermouth

Top with soda water (club soda)

Ice: cube ice

Garnish: a skewered olive (optional) and an orange wedge

EQUIPMENT

Glassware: Highball glass

Jigger

Bar spoon

METHOD

Add all the ingredients to your glass. Add ice and stir. Garnish with an olive and an orange wedge.

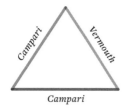

THE HUGO

Cocktails are all about the memories and I will always remember trying my first Hugo at a friend's wedding in Tuscany. The sun was setting over the amazing hilly landscape, and it was the perfect pre-dinner drink. It's an excellent one to scale up into pitchers or a punch bowl for entertaining.

INGREDIENTS

30 ml (1 oz) elderflower liqueur

60 ml (2 oz) sparkling wine

30 ml (1 oz) soda water (club soda)

5 mint leaves

3–4 lemon and lime wheels

Ice: cube ice

Garnish: mint sprig

EQUIPMENT

Glassware: wine glass

Jigger

Bar spoon

METHOD

Add all the ingredients to your glass. Add ice and stir, suspending the mint leaves and citrus wheels through the drink. Garnish with a mint sprig.

Elderflower Liqueur / Elderflower Liqueur / Sparkling Wine

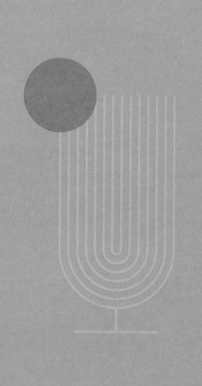

TROPICAL
AND FUN

Cocktails are the holiday we can always afford. Nothing transports you from the humdrum like a brightly coloured, tropical libation. These drinks are often quite complicated with the strong, sweet and bitter/sour elements being split across multiple ingredients to pack a real flavour punch. The undisputed Godfather of this style of drink is Donn Beach (and yes, he did change his name to suit!). He took inspiration from his travels through the Caribbean and South Pacific and served up cocktails laced with tropical fruits and spices, such as nutmeg, allspice and cinnamon. The other main player here was Trader Vic, whose drinks tend to be less complicated than Donn's, but still incredibly flavourful.

This style of drink spent a while out in the wilderness – a proliferation of low-quality knock offs made them seem tacky, but the modern bartending obsession with fresh fruit juices and quality ingredients has given them a new lease of life. Unfortunately, though, it also prompted a resurfacing of a lot of the iconography that surrounded this trend. 'Tiki' is actually a Maori word, denoting a figure similar to Adam in Christian mythology. It expanded to cover totems and carved figures of gods and ancestors – basically, the kind of artefacts that deserve a lot more respect than to be a vessel for fruity cocktails. Given that a lot of these religions, customs and languages died out due to colonisation, it seems insensitive at best to apply them in such a frivolous and kitschy way. So, while the Beachcomber and Trader's influence on this genre of drinks is huge, we cocktail enthusiasts should apply our creativity to move past the tired tropes of a bygone era and make sure this category of drinks is inclusive to all – because they're delicious!

Low and No:

These drinks really come into their own as non-alcoholic options as they are packed full of flavour even without the booze! You may have to adjust the acid either by using shrubs or just increasing the citrus to avoid them becoming too sweet – you still want the drink to taste grown-up! A lot of these drinks contain a LOT of booze – don't be afraid to just cut back the measurements to keep them lower in alcohol.

THE ZOMBIE

The Zombie was one of the earliest drinks served at Don the Beachcomber – Donn Beach's 'tiki shack'. It really exemplified his more-is-more approach to drinks – multiple rums, juices, syrups and liqueurs, it's not subtle! There are many recipe variations out there (even Donn mixed it up throughout his career) so don't be afraid to experiment and use what you have to hand – as long as you keep some tart and sour elements in there it will be delicious. This recipe comes from Jeff 'Beachbum' Berry, an authority on all things tiki, and is meant to be the original 1930s one. This is a BIG drink – Donn limited customers to two a night, which is probably wise.

Ingredients Notes:
[1] *Jamaican rums are big and funky, they have a savoury edge to them. You can absolutely substitute something else in this mould.*

[2] *Puerto Rican rums are lighter in body. You can absolutely substitute something else in this mould.*

[3] *Pro tip: Using a bitters dasher is the easiest way to measure this.*

INGREDIENTS

45 ml (1½ oz) Jamaican aged rum[1]

45 ml (1½ oz) Puerto Rican aged rum[2]

30 ml (1 oz) overproof rum

⅛ teaspoon Herbsaint or Pernod[3]

25 ml (¾ oz) fresh lime juice

15 ml (½ oz) Donn's mix[4]

15 ml (½ oz) falernum syrup

5 ml (⅛ oz) grenadine

1 dash Angostura bitters

Ice: blended or crushed, or a small cube ice

Garnish: mint sprig

EQUIPMENT

Glassware: novelty or Highball glass

Jigger

A blender OR shaker tin

METHOD

If blending, add everything to your blender with a cup of ice and blitz for around 5 seconds (for more on blending drinks, see page 60). If you don't have a blender, add everything to your shaker tin, add ice and shake. 'Dump' the contents of your shaker tin into your glass – i.e. you don't have to strain. Add more ice, if necessary, to fill the glass and garnish.

⁴ Donn had many mixes, designed to stop people stealing his recipes as the bartenders wouldn't know exactly what was in them. According to Beachbum Berry, this one is 1 part cinnamon syrup to 2 parts grapefruit juice.

FOG CUTTER

You'd be forgiven for thinking that rum has a monopoly, but tropical drinks aren't all about this spirit – it shares the stage here. In the same complicated mould as the Zombie, the Fog Cutter has plenty of ingredients, including sherry, which adds an interesting nutty edge. As its creator Trader Vic said, 'Fog Cutter, hell. After two of these you won't even see the stuff'.

Ingredients Note:
[1] A rum agricole works really well here, or another light and grassy light rum.

INGREDIENTS

45 ml (1½ oz) light rum[1]

15 ml (½ oz) brandy

15 ml (½ oz) gin

60 ml (2 oz) freshly squeezed orange juice

30 ml (1 oz) fresh lemon juice

15 ml (½ oz) orgeat

15 ml (½ oz) amontillado sherry

Ice: cube ice

Garnish: mint sprig

EQUIPMENT

Glassware: novelty or Highball glass

Jigger

Shaker tin

Bar spoon

Hawthorne strainer

METHOD

Add everything, except the sherry, to your shaker tin, add ice and shake. Strain into your glass and add fresh ice. Float the sherry on top by pouring over the back of your bar spoon. Garnish with a mint sprig.

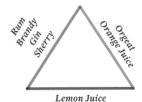

Rum
Brandy
Gin
Sherry

Orgeat
Orange Juice

Lemon Juice

JUNGLEBIRD

Invented in Kuala Lumpur in the 1970s, I love the Junglebird for proving that Campari isn't only for stirred-down and boozy drinks. As tropical as it gets, it is bright, fruity and joyful. The garnish is lots of fun but obviously not necessary if you don't have all the ingredients!

Ingredients Note:
[1] *I actually prefer long-life pineapple juice here for the sweetness – if you use fresh you may have to adjust the sugar.*

INGREDIENTS

45 ml (1½ oz) aged rum

45 ml (1½ oz) pineapple juice[1]

15 ml (½ oz) Campari

15 ml (½ oz) fresh lime juice

10 ml (⅓ oz) cane sugar syrup, or to taste

Ice: cube ice

Garnish: pineapple and a cherry 'bird' (see method)

EQUIPMENT

Glassware: novelty or Highball glass

Jigger

Shaker tin

Hawthorne strainer

METHOD

Prepare your garnish by cutting a triangular wedge of pineapple and trimming a few pineapple fronds. Arrange the fronds on top of each other, then skewer through the cherry, the wedge and the fronds. Fan the fronds out so they look like the tail of a . . . jungle bird! Add everything to your shaker tin, add ice and shake. Strain into your glass and add fresh ice. Crown with your pineapple bird garnish.

Rum / Pineapple Juice / Sugar Syrup

Campari
Lime Juice

THE FAMOUS ONE

MAI TAI

Donn and Trader Vic both claim credit for this drink, with Donn saying Trader Vic ripped off one of his creations and Trader Vic vehemently denying it. This recipe is very much Trader Vic's original take, invented in 1944. Don's drinks are notoriously complicated whereas Vic's original Mai Tai is tight, sharp and well balanced. The name Mai Tai apparently comes from the exclamation of one of Trader Vic's Polynesian friends when he presented them with the drink: Maita'i roa a'e means 'out of this world'!

Ingredients Note:
[1] Rich means that the syrup is made with 2 parts sugar to 1 part water, as opposed to the usual equal parts.

INGREDIENTS

60 ml (2 oz) aged rum

25 ml (¾ oz) fresh lime juice

15 ml (½ oz) curaçao

10 ml (⅓ oz) orgeat

5–10 ml (⅙–⅓ oz) rich demerara sugar syrup[1] (see page 44)

Ice: cube ice

Garnish: mint sprig and a lime husk

EQUIPMENT

Glassware: novelty or rocks glass

Jigger

Shaker tin

METHOD

Add everything to your shaker tin, add ice and shake. 'Dump' the contents of your shaker tin into your glass – i.e. you don't have to strain. Add more ice, if necessary, to fill the glass and garnish, arranging your lime husk and mint sprig to look like a desert island and a palm tree – cute!

⌣

THE HURRICANE

The story of the Hurricane (not the Dylan song) is pretty well accepted. It was born at Pat O'Brien's bar in New Orleans in the 1940s out of a surplus of rum. This cocktail is probably one of the most misunderstood – it is often served with at least two more ingredients than necessary but it's really more of a Rum Sour. That said, it is pretty boozy, so if you would like to lengthen it out, then I'd say to stick 30 ml (1 oz) of either freshly squeezed orange juice or pineapple juice.

INGREDIENTS

40 ml (1⅓ oz) light rum

40 ml (1⅓ oz) aged rum

30 ml (1 oz) passionfruit syrup

30 ml (1 oz) fresh lemon juice

Ice: crushed or cube ice

Garnish: orange wedge and a cherry – and a cocktail umbrella if you feel like it!

EQUIPMENT

Glassware: the Hurricane glass is where it gets its name, but bear in mind these are usually huge – the original recipe was actually 4 full shots of rum!

Jigger

Shaker tin (if no crushed ice)

METHOD

Add everything to your glass, add crushed ice and churn. Alternatively, if you don't have crushed ice and feel too lazy to make some (which is usually me), add your ingredients to your shaker tin, add ice and shake. 'Dump' the contents of your shaker tin into your glass – i.e. you don't have to strain. Add more ice, if necessary, to fill the glass and garnish with a skewered orange wedge and cherry.

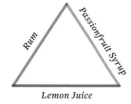

⌣

ARTICHOKE HOLD

This is a very modern classic – it was only invented in 2019 by Jeremy Oertel at now-closed bar Donna in New York. I love it because it hits strong, sweet, sour AND bitter – all the bases!

Ingredients Note:
¹ Cynar is an amaro that uses artichoke as a botanical – hence the name of the cocktail!

INGREDIENTS

20 ml (¾ oz) aged rum

5 ml (⅛ oz) overproof rum

25 ml (¾ oz) Cynar[1]

15 ml (½ oz) elderflower liqueur

15 ml (½ oz) orgeat

20 ml (⅔ oz) fresh lime juice

Ice: cubes

Garnish: mint sprig

EQUIPMENT

Glassware: novelty or rocks glass

Jigger

Shaker tin

METHOD

Add everything to your shaker tin, add ice and shake. 'Dump' the contents of your shaker tin into your glass – i.e. you don't have to strain. Add more ice, if necessary, to fill the glass and garnish with a mint sprig.

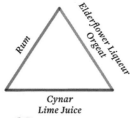

Rum — Elderflower Liqueur — Orgeat

Cynar
Lime Juice

PIÑA COLADA

This is a shaken Piña Colada, but it is very easily adapted to a frozen drink (see page 171). There are actually two bars in Puerto Rico that bear a plaque proclaiming themselves to be the birthplace of this legendary beverage – the Caribe Hilton's Beachcomber Bar and the Barrachina restaurant. There's even a pirate who gets some credit too. Realistically, the simple combination of rum, coconut and pineapple has been played with in the kinds of tropical places that are home to all three since rum was invented, but it does seem to be the Caribe Hilton that combined the name Piña Colada and the drink we know now. Making coconut cream had always been a labour-intensive process, but in the 1950s Coco Lopez hit the market (which is a canned and sweetened coconut cream) and so it became more viable for high-volume bars to use it in drinks – at the Caribe they started adding it to their Piña Fria, which was just rum and pineapple, and named the new concoction the Piña Colada, which means 'strained pineapple'.

Ingredients Note:
[1] Freshly squeezed is great but long-life pineapple juice also makes a delicious drink.

INGREDIENTS

60 ml (2 oz) aged rum

60 ml (2 oz) pineapple juice[1]

30 ml (1 oz) sweetened coconut cream

Ice: cube ice or crushed

Garnish: a fruit wedge and a cocktail cherry, a skewer or cocktail umbrella

EQUIPMENT

Glassware: novelty or Highball glass

Jigger

Shaker tin

Hawthorne strainer

Fine strainer

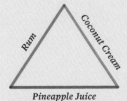

METHOD

Add all the ingredients to your shaker tin, add ice and shake – this helps aerate the coconut cream. Double-strain (to help preserve the fluffy texture) and add fresh ice (you can use crushed if you prefer). Garnish tropically, and enjoy!

PAINKILLER

This 1970s creation from the Soggy Dollar Bar in the British Virgin Islands (so named because there's no dock, so patrons have to swim ashore, wetting their wallets in the process) is essentially just a Piña Colada with added juiciness from the orange and spice from the nutmeg.

INGREDIENTS

60 ml (2 oz) dark rum

120 ml (4 oz) pineapple juice

30 ml (1 oz) orange juice

30 ml (1 oz) sweetened coconut cream

Ice: cube ice or crushed

Garnish: grated nutmeg and a pineapple wedge

EQUIPMENT

Glassware: novelty or Highball glass

Jigger

Shaker tin

Hawthorne strainer

Fine strainer

Microplane

METHOD

Add all the ingredients to your shaker tin, add ice and shake – this helps aerate the coconut cream. Double-strain (to help preserve the fluffy texture) and add fresh ice (you can use crushed if you prefer). Grate nutmeg over the top and garnish with a pineapple wedge.

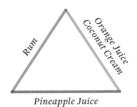
Rum
Orange Juice
Coconut Cream
Pineapple Juice

⌣

THE LOLA

This zingy number is a favourite of mine from an old workplace –
Union Electric Bar in Melbourne.

Ingredients Notes:
¹ Should be something quite dry.

² To make this extra spicy, the crew at Union Electric juice fresh ginger and blend with sugar syrup. Otherwise you can just infuse ginger in sugar syrup, then strain as usual, but leave in for a little longer to make sure it has some bite.

INGREDIENTS

45 ml (1½ oz) gin

30 ml (1 oz) sweetened coconut cream

15 ml (½ oz) curaçao[1]

7.5 ml (¼ oz) ginger syrup[2]

Ice: cube ice

Garnish: cracked black pepper, orange zest twist (see page 75) and a pineapple frond

EQUIPMENT

Glassware: rocks glass

Jigger

Shaker tin

METHOD

Add all the ingredients to your shaker tin and shake hard. 'Dump' into your rocks glass (i.e. you don't have to strain) and garnish.

FROZEN MARGARITA

Cocktail lore is usually pretty imprecise to say the least, but in this case the inventor, Mariano Martinez, has had the history codified by the Smithsonian Museum. When Mariano opened a Mexican restaurant he put frozen Margaritas on the menu, but his bartender struggled to keep up with demand and the quality of the drinks was nowhere near what it should have been. But then, the eureka moment – while stopping at a 7-Eleven he saw the Slurpees and thought, why don't I premix my Margaritas in a slushie machine?! After a fair bit of tinkering on a second-hand soft-serve machine, and on the recipe itself to get the right texture, on 11 May 1971 he pulled the lever to pour the very first frozen Margy into a glass, and the US has never looked back.

Pro Tip: How to Make Great Frozen Drinks

1. *Temperature. Everything has to be cold when it goes in the blender, and your glass should be chilled in the freezer if at all possible.*

2. *Ice. Use smaller cubes or crushed ice, about 1 cup per drink.*

3. *Balance. The cold numbs your flavour receptors so you will need more sweetness than usual, and can get away with more bitterness.*

4. *Alcohol by volume (ABV). To get the correct texture, the alcohol level has to be correct. Too high and it won't freeze, too low and it will freeze too solidly.*

5. *Straws. You need nice wide ones for easy suction!*

INGREDIENTS

45 ml (1½ oz) blanco tequila

20 ml (⅔ oz) orange liqueur

15 ml (½ oz) sugar syrup (see page 44)

20 ml (⅔ oz) fresh lime juice

1 cup ice

Served up (no ice)

Garnish: salt rim and a lime wheel

EQUIPMENT

Glassware: large coupe or Martini glass

Jigger

Blender

METHOD

Have your glass frozen, run a lime wedge around the side and dab in salt, shaking off any excess. Have all the ingredients chilled and add them to the blender, working as quickly as possible. Add the ice and blend, starting slowly then going to full speed. Don't whizz for too long as you don't want your drink starting to heat up from the friction. Pour into your glass, garnish with a lime wheel and enjoy!

FROZEN STRAWBERRY DAIQUIRI

The Frozen Strawberry Daiquiri actually has a rather venerable history as far as modern frozen cocktails go. Crushed ice was being added to Daiquiris at El Floridita in Cuba as far back as the 1930s, and when the blender was popularised by Fred Waring in 1938, he took it to a famed 'home economist' (Mabel Stegner) who then included a Strawberry Daiquiri in her 1952 book *Electric Blender Recipes*.

Ingredients Note:
[1] To make a strawberry fan, using a sharp knife make slits in a strawberry from just below the stem to the other side, so the strawberry is held together at the stem end. Fan out the slices.

INGREDIENTS

60 ml (2 oz) light rum

30 ml (1 oz) sugar syrup (see page 44)

30 ml (1 oz) fresh lime juice

4–5 frozen strawberries

1 cup ice

Served up (no ice)

Garnish: strawberry fan[1]

EQUIPMENT

Glassware: large coupe or Martini glass

Blender

METHOD

Have all the ingredients chilled and add them to the blender, working as quickly as possible. Add your ice and blend, starting slowly then going to full speed. Don't whizz for too long as you don't want your drink starting to heat up from the friction. Pour into your glass, garnish with a strawberry fan and enjoy!

175

BOOZY GRANITA

If you don't fancy being chained to a blender all night, try this option, which can be prepared ahead of time. It is really adaptable – try different juices and liqueurs. This recipe makes about six servings – it can be scaled up or down.

INGREDIENTS

100 ml (3 oz) fresh grapefruit juice

100 ml (3 oz) fresh orange juice

200 ml (6 oz) white vermouth

100 ml (3 oz) peach liqueur

100 ml (3 oz) water

30 ml (1 oz) gin per glass when serving (optional but recommended)

1 cup ice

Served up (no ice)

Garnish: mint sprig and a grapefruit wedge

EQUIPMENT

Glassware: sundae or rocks glass

Freezer-friendly bowl

Measuring jug

Jigger

METHOD

Add everything to the bowl, except the gin, and freeze – preferably overnight. Remove from the fridge and gently flake with a fork. Add a shot of gin to each glass and scoop the granita on top. Garnish with a mint sprig and a grapefruit wedge, add a straw or spoon (or both!) and enjoy!

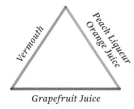

177

WILDCARDS AND WEIRDOS

I've always had a soft spot for oddballs and these drinks don't like
being put in boxes. That said though, they do still follow some rules –
as much as they may look a little different, they all still have the Taste
Triangle as the base. It's just that their sweet and bitter or sour might be
coming from some slightly unorthodox places, such as coffee or dairy!
From savoury hangover cures to dessert cocktails, these drinks really
stretch the bounds of flavour.

COBBLERS
AND JULEPS

This chapter is about the mavericks, and Juleps and Cobblers are some of the earliest mixed drinks. I have grouped them together due to their similar serves, and you can play around with the base, fruit and herbs for infinite variations.

Low and No:

There are such strong flavours at play in most of these cocktails that the booze components can easily be skipped or cut back. Fortified wines work well as substitutes in many of them (or are already the base) for a lower-alcohol option.

MINT JULEP

Thought to have originated in the 1700s, the first written reference to the Julep was in 1803, three years before the word 'cocktail' was even defined, and is thought to have been why the straw was invented. As much as it is synonymous with Kentucky nowadays, it seems it was actually a Virginian invention, and was often based on fruit brandies rather than bourbon. Its popularity spread as ice became more widely available – what better way to cool down on a hot afternoon in the South than with a mound of frosty crushed ice in your whiskey, while the metal cup keeps everything cold? In 1938 it became the official drink of the Kentucky Derby, where an unholy amount is now consumed every year. As much as it is served on crushed ice, this drink is actually more akin to an Old Fashioned than a Mojito – you're supposed to taste the bourbon!

Ingredients Note:
[1] These are not traditional but the addition of any bitters makes it a much better drink (in my opinion!).

INGREDIENTS

4–5 mint leaves

10 ml (⅔ oz) sugar syrup (see page 44)

60 ml (2 oz) bourbon

2 dashes peach bitters[1]

Ice: crushed

Garnish: mint sprig

EQUIPMENT

Glassware: silver Julep cup or rocks glass

Tea towel (dish towel)

Mallet or rolling pin

Jigger

Bar spoon

METHOD

Of course this drink is much easier if you have access to a crushed ice machine! If not, take out some frustrations by wrapping cube ice in a tea towel and bashing with a mallet or rolling pin. Gently muddle the mint leaves in the sugar syrup, then add the bourbon and peach bitters. Fill with crushed ice and churn until the cup frosts. Cap with more crushed ice and garnish with a mint sprig. A straw is necessary too!

SHERRY COBBLER

Like the Mint Julep, the Cobbler's rise in popularity was closely linked to the spread of commercial ice. With the base being wine, though, these drinks are a much more sensible choice on a hot afternoon than whisk(e)y! It is widely accepted that the Sherry Cobbler was the first ever shaken cocktail, and is actually where the cobbler shaker gets its name from!

Ingredients Notes:
[1] *Sugar syrup is traditional but I like to stick with the sherry theme.*

[2] *I like to use a fruity or nutty bitters.*

INGREDIENTS

2 wedges orange

2 wedges lemon

60 ml (2 oz) amontillado sherry

15 ml (½ oz) Pedro Ximénez sherry[1]

1 dash bitters (optional)[2]

Ice: crushed

Garnish: mint sprig, fresh berries and white granulated sugar

EQUIPMENT

Glassware: goblet or rocks glass

Jigger

Shaker tin

Hawthorne strainer

Bar spoon

Straw

METHOD

Squeeze the wedges of fruit into your shaker tin. Add the sherries and bitters to your shaker tin, fill with ice and shake hard! Strain over crushed ice, or an easy fix is to 'shake and dump' – i.e. don't strain at all but pour the entire contents of your shaker into the glass if you don't have crushed ice. The broken-up ice gives the effect you're after. Use your bar spoon to suspend the wedges through the drink. Garnish with mint and fresh fruit, dust with sugar and – it must be served with a straw.

Amontillado Sherry

PX Sherry
Orange

Lemon
Bitters

THE BRAMBLE

This seems like it should have been around forever, but is actually a modern classic, created by Dick Bradsell in the 1980s. I think of it as a modernised version of a Cobbler, with more citrus but the same verve and fruitiness.

INGREDIENTS

60 ml (2 oz) gin

30 ml (1 oz) fresh lemon juice

10 ml (⅓ oz) sugar syrup
(see page 44)

15 ml (½ oz) crème de mûre

Ice: crushed

Garnish: lemon wheel and
blackberries

EQUIPMENT

Glassware: rocks

Jigger

Shaker tin

Hawthorne strainer

Bar spoon

METHOD

Add all the ingredients, except the crème de mûre, to your shaker tin, shake and either strain over crushed ice or 'dump' into the glass (i.e. don't strain). Drizzle the crème de mûre over the back of a bar spoon into the drink. Garnish with a lemon wheel and some fresh blackberries.

CREAMY DRINKS

Dessert cocktails can be a danger zone – I'll keep the chocolate and caramel syrups for my ice cream, thanks! These drinks manage to be indulgent while surprisingly light and well-balanced with acid coming from dairy and/or fortified wine.

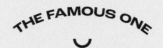

THE ALEXANDER

The Alexander is another Grandfather cocktail, having been around since the 1910s, and was actually originally made using gin! This cocktail first appeared in print in 1916 but the origins are apparently pretty steamy . . . no, not that kind of steamy. The Delaware, Lackawanna and Western Railroad were very proud of the fact that they used 'clean' coal and advertised this fact with a lady called Phoebe Snow, whose white dress remained pristine when she journeyed on their railroad. When they booked an event at a trendy New York restaurant, the bartender there wanted to create a pure white cocktail in homage, and so shook up some gin, crème de cacao and cream. It really took hold during Prohibition as the creaminess conveniently masked the harsh bathtub gin. Where exactly the brandy came in is a mystery, but it has stuck and is arguably more popular than its gin counterpart.

Ingredients Note:
[1] The original recipe is just a full 30 ml (1 oz) of crème de cacao, but I like the bitter edge from adding a little coffee liqueur. You could also add a dash of cocktail bitters.

INGREDIENTS

30 ml (1 oz) gin or brandy

15 ml (½ oz) crème de cacao

15 ml (½ oz) coffee liqueur[1]

30 ml (1 oz) cream

Served up (no ice)

Garnish: grated nutmeg

EQUIPMENT

Glassware: coupe

Jigger

Shaker tin

Hawthorne strainer

Fine strainer

Microplane

METHOD

Add all the ingredients to your shaker tin, add ice and shake hard – you want to make it nice and airy. Double-strain into a chilled coupe glass and grate nutmeg on top.

Brandy Gin

Crème de Cacao

Cream
Coffee Liqueur

EGGNOG

This is part of the Flip family (which contain whole eggs for a creamy texture), one of the oldest styles of cocktails. Traditionally drunk around Christmas time, a properly made Eggnog is actually much lighter than store-bought versions, so I find it a great after-dinner treat at any time of the year!

INGREDIENTS

Ingredients Notes:
[1] Try not to use something overly sweet, or adjust the sugar accordingly.

[2] If you prefer boozier, you could use brandy instead, or just go 2 shots of rum.

30 ml (1 oz) spiced rum[1]

30 ml (1 oz) ruby port or similar dessert wine[2]

20 ml (⅔ oz) sugar syrup (see page 44)

20 ml (⅔ oz) cream

1 whole egg

Served up (no ice)

Garnish: nutmeg

EQUIPMENT

Glassware: coupe

Jigger

Shaker tin

Hawthorne strainer

Fine strainer

Microplane

METHOD

Add all the ingredients to your shaker tin and dry-shake. Once everything has emulsified, fill your shaker tin with as much ice as possible and shake hard. Pop the tin open and double-strain into your chilled coupe glass. Grate nutmeg on top to garnish.

COFFEE COCKTAIL

Despite the name, this cocktail does not in fact contain coffee. Instead, the egg gives it the texture and colour of a creamy coffee.

INGREDIENTS

30 ml (1 oz) brandy

30 ml (1 oz) ruby port

20 ml (⅔ oz) sugar syrup (see page 44)

1 whole egg

Served up (no ice)

Garnish: nutmeg

EQUIPMENT

Glassware: coupe

Jigger

Shaker tin

Hawthorne strainer

Fine strainer

Microplane

METHOD

Add all the ingredients to your shaker tin, then dry-shake. Once everything has emulsified, fill your shaker tin with as much ice as possible and shake hard. Pop the tin open and double-strain into your chilled coupe glass. Grate nutmeg on top to garnish.

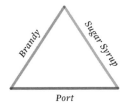

COFFEE
DRINKS

Coffee is a great cocktail ingredient, bringing its own acid and bitterness.

THE FAMOUS ONE

ESPRESSO MARTINI

The Espresso Martini was invented in London in 1983. The story goes that a – never named, but apparently now mega famous – model walked up to Dick Bradsell's bar and asked for a drink that would wake her up and f*ck her up. He obliged by shaking up vodka, fresh espresso, coffee liqueur and sugar syrup. The result was a frothy, bittersweet miracle, which I'm sure got both jobs done! He initially called it the Vodka Espresso, then the Pharmaceutical Stimulant (which is actually my favourite title) but, as with most drinks of that era served in a Martini glass, it couldn't escape the 'Martini' moniker and this is how it's now known worldwide. Australia, with its booming coffee culture, really embraced the Espresso Martini and I probably make more of them than any other cocktail.

Ingredients Note:
[1] *Split a vanilla pod and leave to infuse in sugar syrup overnight.*

INGREDIENTS

45 ml (1½ oz) vodka

30 ml (1 oz) espresso or cold brew concentrate

20 ml (⅔ oz) coffee liqueur

5 ml (⅙ oz) vanilla syrup (optional)[1]

Served up (no ice)

Garnish: lemon zest twist (see page 75; optional) and 3 coffee beans

EQUIPMENT

Glassware: coupe or Martini glass

Jigger

Shaker tin

Hawthorne strainer

Fine strainer

METHOD

Add all the ingredients to your shaker tin, add ice and shake hard. Double-strain into a chilled coupe glass, fold your lemon zest over the top to expel the oils, then discard, then float three coffee beans on the fluffy head (they represent health, wealth and happiness).

⌣

IRISH COFFEE

The Irish Coffee was invented by chef Joe Sheridan at an airport restaurant near Limerick, Ireland in the 1940s, in the days when transatlantic flights were made on flying boats and often had to turn back due to inclement weather. The weary passengers needed to warm up, so Sheridan spiked their coffees with some local whiskey and topped it with cream. One passenger apparently asked if he had used Brazilian coffee, to which he got the reply 'no, it was an Irish coffee' accompanied, at least in my head, by a cheeky Irish wink.

Ingredients Note:
[1] At home I usually use a coffee plunger. Espresso coffee can work but it's a little more bitter.

INGREDIENTS

Roughly 120 ml (4 oz) filter coffee[1]

Roughly 90 ml (3 oz) cream

45 ml (1½ oz) blended Irish whiskey

15 ml (½ oz) brown sugar syrup (see page 44)

Served up (no ice)

Garnish: none

EQUIPMENT

Glassware: glass coffee cup

Jigger

Shaker tin

Bar spoon

A Hawthorne strainer coil

Coffee making equipment (e.g., cafetière)

METHOD

Add hot water to your glass to warm it up. Brew your coffee. To whip the cream, pour it into your shaker tin, and remove the coil from your Hawthorne strainer and pop that in too. Shake hard for a minute or two until the cream is whipped. Add the coffee to the glass first to retain the heat, then add the whiskey and sugar syrup. Give it all a stir, then turn your bar spoon over and slowly pour the whipped cream over the back of it. It should float nicely on top to create a creamy, Guinness-esque head.

Whiskey · *Sugar Syrup*

Cream Coffee

WHITE RUSSIAN

Not exactly a little-known twist, but it had to be included. As simple as this drink is, it is one of the highest-viewed videos on the Behind the Bar YouTube channel. The Dude abides, and so does this cocktail.

Ingredients Note:
[1] *The original recipe calls for cream, although many people will make it with milk, which obviously makes it less rich.*

INGREDIENTS

30 ml (1 oz) vodka

20 ml (⅔ oz) coffee liqueur

30 ml (1 oz) cream[1]

Ice: large block or cube ice

Garnish: nutmeg

EQUIPMENT

Glassware: rocks glass

Jigger

Microplane

METHOD

Add the vodka and liqueur to your glass and add a large ice cube. Slowly pour the cream in over the ice if you want to create a layered effect, otherwise just add the cream with everything else. Grate a little nutmeg over the top.

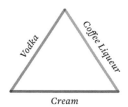

Vodka — Coffee Liqueur — Cream

SAVOURY
DRINKS

We've talked a lot about sweet, sour and bitter but everyone needs a bit
of umami in their life every now and again!

BLOODY MARY

The man usually credited with the Bloody Mary is Fernand Petiot, a French-born bartender at Harry's New York Bar in Paris. The story goes that the revolution in Russia had forced many Russians to flee, and they fled holding their bottles of vodka, introducing it wherever they ended up – including Paris. Fernand had been trying to figure out how to use this new spirit, and canned tomato juice was also a new invention, so he combined the two with some seasonings in a stroke of mad genius. There is also a claim from comedian George Jessel, who says he mixed vodka and tomato juice in the kind of inspiration that only strikes when you're still awake at 8 am after a night of drinking. What's most likely is that the combination of vodka and tomato juice existed (whether invented by Jessel or not), but Petiot was the one who spiced it up and put it on the map. As for the name, it could be after a British monarch, a waitress at a disreputable saloon, a jilted lover or a socialite in a white dress . . . choose your contender!

197

INGREDIENTS

60 ml (2 oz) vodka[1]

Large pinch celery salt

Large pinch cracked black pepper

6 dashes Tabasco, or to taste

20 ml (⅔ oz) Worcestershire sauce

15 ml (½ oz) fresh lemon juice

90 ml (3 oz) tomato juice

5–10 ml (⅙–⅓ oz) manzanilla sherry

Ice: cube ice

Garnish: herbs (I like rosemary and thyme) and celery (although I don't like it so I use an olive!)

EQUIPMENT

Glassware: Highball glass

Jigger

Shaker tin

Julep strainer

Ingredients Note:
[1] I'm a fan of substituting in blanco tequila for a Bloody Maria, or use gin for a Red Snapper. The Bloody Mary is very personalisable. I like to add a little dry sherry, some people prefer a little sweetness from something like maple syrup to balance it out. You can obviously adjust all of these proportions to your own taste for spice and salinity.

METHOD

Add all the ingredients, except the sherry, to your shaker tin and fill with ice. Use your julep strainer to hold the ice back in one half of the tin and pour your cocktail into the other half of the tin. Do this back and forth about five times! If this sounds a bit scary or you have cream carpets, try sealing the tin as usual but just gently rolling the tin around, instead of shaking. Strain over fresh ice and float the manzanilla sherry on top, then garnish.

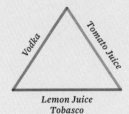

Vodka / Tomato Juice / Lemon Juice / Tobasco

MICHELADA

The word Michelada is a portmanteau, which loosely translates as 'my cold beer'. Apparently, a man named Michel Esper Jorge from Mexico was a bit hungover one day and started throwing some seasonings and lime juice into his beer in a quest for refreshment. This drink has since taken on a life of its own. In Mexico a Michelada is often just a beer, lime and a salt rim, with maybe a dash of Maggi Seasoning or Tabasco. Here in Australia, tomato juice is often added and, since that's the one I was introduced to, that's what I've included here – it is very heavily seasoned so feel free to cut back!

INGREDIENTS

15 ml (½ oz) fresh lime juice

15 ml (½ oz) mezcal (optional)

60 ml (2 oz) tomato juice (optional)

30 ml (1 oz) Maggi Seasoning

15 ml (½ oz) Worcestershire sauce

10 ml (⅓ oz) agave syrup

5 dashes Tabasco or other hot sauce, or to taste

Pinch cracked black pepper, or to taste

Mexican lager to top

Ice: cube ice

Garnish: Tajin seasoning or salt rim

EQUIPMENT

Glassware: pint glass or other large glass

Jigger

A barspoon

METHOD

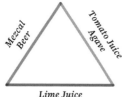

Mezcal
Beer

Tomato Juice
Agave

Lime Juice
Tabasco

This drink can just be built as the fizzy lager does all the aerating for you, but you have to keep everything as cold as you can – definitely keep the glass in the freezer if possible and, if you're making a lot, I'd suggest batching all your seasoning and keeping that chilled as well. Rim your glass by running a lime wedge around the outside then dab in Tajin seasoning or salt and shake off any excess. Add all the ingredients, except the beer, to your glass, then fill with beer to about halfway. Top with ice and serve with the rest of the beer on the side – it can be added gradually to lessen the seasoning intensity.

FUN TWIST

⌣

TENDRIL LOVIN'

When using seasonal ingredients in cocktails it's fun to think outside the box – using vegetables rather than just fruits in drinks adds an interesting edge. This is a savoury Daiquiri twist I came up with, inspired by a cocktail I tried and loved at the beginning of my bartending career (unfortunately I don't remember the name, but it lives on in my obsession with using peas in drinks!).

Ingredients Note:
[1] A really crisp and grassy white rum works best. Add around 10 snow peas to a bottle and allow to infuse for 48 hours before straining.

INGREDIENTS

45 ml (1½ oz) snow pea (mangetout)–infused light rum[1]

20 ml (⅔ oz) dry vermouth

5 ml (⅙ oz) falernum syrup

5 ml (⅙ oz) sugar syrup (see page 44)

20 ml (⅔ oz) fresh lime juice

Served up (no ice)

Garnish: pea tendril

EQUIPMENT

Glassware: coupe or Martini glass

Jigger

Shaker tin

Hawthorne strainer

Fine strainer

METHOD

Add all the ingredients to your shaker tin, add ice and shake.
Double strain into a chilled coupe glass and garnish with a pea tendril.

Rum — Vermouth Falernum Sugar Syrup — Lime Juice

AFTERWORD

A true host doesn't get lost in the minutiae.
She keeps her head up, tells stories, makes
people feel at home, adjusts drinks and
surroundings to her guests' tastes, whether in
a world-renowned cocktail bar, the local pub or
her own kitchen.

I hope this book has helped expand your
repertoire. So many cocktails are just
variations on the blueprint of another cocktail,
and when you add in your own personal flair
the possibilities are limitless.

So, now you know.

ACKNOWLEDGEMENTS

Some of my earliest memories are of dining out with my family – getting dressed up for a birthday meal at the fancy Chinese restaurant in town; high tea or cheese toasties by the seaside on holidays; the local Indian most Fridays. So thank you Mum and Dad for instilling a love of food and drink in me from an early age, and for not disowning me when I decided to become a bartender instead of a lawyer (hopefully this book makes up for it a little!). Thank you also to my awesome sister and friends back home in Scotland for your enthusiasm for this project from the get-go. Yes, you all get signed copies.

I wouldn't be in the position to write this book if it wasn't for my hospitality career, so thank you to everyone who has had an influence on that, whether I've worked alongside you or been propped up at your bar too often. In particular, the Melbourne hospitality community is such an inspiring thing to be a part of – I'm not sure this would have happened in any other city. Thank you to Jesse, Kelly, Shane and Andrew for taking a punt on a random Scot who came in demanding to stay in the country, and for continuing to help me forge a rewarding path in this industry (extra props to Jesse for helping tee up the book deal!). Thank you to the Bomba crew, especially Hannah and Lindsay, for holding down the fort while I was trying to get this done and managing to keep your eye-rolling to a minimum when it was all I could talk about for a while.

Of course, I have a debt of gratitude to everyone who has watched my videos, especially those who made nice comments! I probably wouldn't have had the confidence to do this without feeling that there is a genuine community behind it. You have proven to me that the internet is not all bad.

Writing a book was a rather daunting task for someone who is more used to penning five-minute YouTube videos and snappy magazine articles, so I very much appreciate the efforts of the team at Hardie Grant for making it all (relatively!) painless – Roxy Ryan for thinking this was a good idea in the first place, Rushani Epa for her patience and cheerfulness and Ariana Klepac for her careful eye. Also to the visuals team – Gareth Sobey, Melinda King and George Saad – who have made the book look better than I could have imagined.

Last, but most certainly not least, I really couldn't have done it without my home team. Thelma, your aggressive kitty cuddles sometimes made typing on a laptop pretty difficult, but they saved me from many a meltdown. And Fred, for your unwavering support of me, your genuine pride in everything I do, your indispensable advice and ability to make me look at things from entirely new angles (or at least pour me a whisky and give me a cuddle until I'm in the headspace to do so) ... I might be able to do it without you, but I sure as hell never want to.

INDEX

Published in 2023 by Hardie Grant Books, an imprint of Hardie Grant Publishing

Hardie Grant Books (Melbourne)
Wurundjeri Country
Building 1, 658 Church Street
Richmond, Victoria 3121

Hardie Grant Books (London)
5th & 6th Floors
52–54 Southwark Street
London SE1 1UN

hardiegrant.com/au/books

Hardie Grant acknowledges the Traditional Owners of the country on which we work, the Wurundjeri people of the Kulin nation and the Gadigal people of the Eora nation, and recognises their continuing connection to the land, waters and culture. We pay our respects to their Elders past and present.

 A catalogue record for this book is available from the National Library of Australia

Strong, Sweet and Bitter
ISBN 978 1 74379 853 9

10 9 8 7 6 5 4 3 2

Publisher: Rushani Epa
Editor: Ariana Klepac
Design Manager: Kristin Thomas
Designer: George Saad
Photographer: Gareth Sobey
Stylist: Melinda King
Production Manager: Todd Rechner
Production Coordinator: Jessica Harvie

Colour reproduction by Splitting Image Colour Studio
Printed in China by Leo Paper Products LTD.

 The paper this book is printed on is from FSC®-certified forests and other sources. FSC® promotes environmentally responsible, socially beneficial and economically viable management of the world's forests.